PINTS OF PORTER
and other essays

PINTS OF PORTER
and other essays

JOHN B. KEANE

Foreword
by
Conor Keane

MERCIER PRESS

MERCIER PRESS
Douglas Village, Cork
www.mercierpress.ie

Trade enquiries to COLUMBA MERCIER DISTRIBUTION,
55a Spruce Avenue, Stillorgan Industrial Park, Blackrock, Dublin

First published 2004
© The Estate of John B. Keane

ISBN: 1 85635 438 5

10 9 8 7 6 5 4 3 2 1

Mercier Press receives financial assistance from
The Arts Council/An Chomhairle Ealaíon, Ireland

the arts
council
schomhairle
ealaíon

Printed in Ireland by ColourBooks Ltd.

Contents

Foreword

Porter and pandy played important roles in the Keane household of my boyhood. The sale of porter in the family bar provided the wherewithal to buy the spuds that were transformed into that glorious and under-rated culinary delight known as pandy. So, it is no surprise that both should feature in this collection of essays which, when originally published in newspapers like the *Limerick Leader* and *Evening Herald*, provided a few more bob to supplement the family's diet.

A publican's lot in a town like Listowel in the 1960s was hard graft. There were close to 70 public houses in a small town with a population of around 3,400. When you take out the 1,500 children who were under drinking age, the 1,000 or so old and infirm, the 500 non-drinkers and the 50 or so nuns and priests, then the 70 publicans were left with a regular drinking population of no more than 350 people or just five drinkers for every pub. It was hard to make ends meet especially when you consider 70 of the 350 drinkers were also publicans.

The pub saw after the pandy, but the essays gave my dad the price of a few pints to help ease his porter tooth. There is a porter tooth in the head of every Keane that was ever born. My father knew this and prepared us in ways unknown to the most gifted orthodontists to deal with this hereditary dental malady. In essence he trained me how to drink, and how to drink porter in particular. But there was really no need to provide me with any instructions on how to drink porter: I was a natural.

The real lessons imparted by my dear departed father were on how to hold my drink, the etiquette of drinking and the dangers of drink. Working behind the counter in a family-run pub provides a great education, one which is not available at any third-level institution; it is a kind of 'Encounter-level' education. One lesson learned quickly is that there are very few nice drunks. Later you learn that drink has the potential to destroy the drinker and his family and often ends in premature death.

Drink was the first weapon of mass destruction I ever encountered, and so I learned to respect it. John B. taught me all this and more. As a teenager I was allowed to drink a few half pints of porter when we travelled to football matches. This brought me into adult drinking company as a neophyte.

On one memorable occasion I was granted an exemption from my apprenticeship. Listowel won the North Kerry Senior Football Championship and I was part of the team while still playing juvenile football. This is as hard a football competition to win as any in the country and there are those with All-Ireland football medals who do not have North Kerry championships. The final was played in Ballylongford, and after the game the Listowel supporters celebrated in the village's lovely pubs while the vanquished Tarbert supporters mingled amongst us in our merriment. It was a great day.

John B. slipped me a generous wad of cash and told me not to be shy of the counter and to drink like a man for the day with my team-mates. As always, I did as I was bid, but my apprenticeship papers were reinstated on our next footballing foray.

The lessons imparted to me by my father as a boy have borne the test of time, as do the essays in the following pages.

CONOR KEANE
Fenit 2004

Pints of Porter

The common pint of porter is one of man's few great allies.

Apart from its known curative and body-building properties, its appearance – when presented properly – is a work of art. The rich creamy head and the black glistening body are its only features but the two combine to charm the eye and stimulate the heart. There are few tonics which possess the restorative constituents of its substance and perhaps the greatest tribute paid to it was by an impecunious old gentleman of my acquaintance when he said: 'I spent most of my money on porter, and the rest of it foolishly'.

The pint of porter is the cheapest form of intoxicating drink and those of God's creatures who cannot abide without it are not to be blamed. They are to be pitied for abusing the virtue of moderation but excused on the grounds that they are not addicted to the smaller but more spirited kinfolk of the pint.

There is no excuse for those who think of it in terms of gallons rather than pints. We hear such expressions as 'He'd sell his soul for porter!' or 'He'd suck porter out of a sore heel!' but perhaps the best description I ever heard of the complete porter addict was once after a wren-dance in North Kerry, when a certain pot-bellied guzzler was reputed to have drunk four gallons between midnight and dawn.

'That man is very fond of porter,' I said to an old woman who was playing a concertina by my side.

'If he was caught by cannibals,' she said, 'and boiled in a

pot, the soup out of his bones would have their children drunk for generations.'

Porter must not be guzzled. It must be savoured and swallowed slowly with the true grin of appreciation and the more hideous the grin the more obvious it should be that the drinker knows the value of well-conditioned porter. Nobody knows when men first started to grin over their porter-drinking but my firm belief is that they first did it to deceive their wives into thinking that porter was contemptible and unfit for the soft lips of their spouses. A very commendable practice indeed and one which reminds me of an old parish priest I once knew. He would lean over the pulpit and say in a low voice, which carried to the four corners of the chapel, 'A drunken man is a drunken man'. Then after a pause he would raise his finger and in a great voice proclaim: 'But a drunken woman is a drunken woman!'

Give me the man who can drink his few pints without commotion and instability, who can be his wife's knight-at-arms, equerry and counsellor after porter, who can astonish her with repartee and comment which she never thought he possessed and who tells her that he loves her as much as he did the first day they met, after porter.

I will always remember a burly giant of a truck-driver from Limerick who, one summer's day, entered my bar and called for a pint of porter. He took his cap from his head and wiped away the perspiration from his forehead. He took the pint and swallowed it without taking the glass from his mouth. He wiped his lips and hoisted his trousers and I swear to you that his sigh of satisfaction could be heard half-way around the world.

Porter was made for men like this man and porter was the due of this man but I will never forget another occasion when a huge blacksmith entered a pub in a small country village. The sweat ran from his forehead and his chest heaved from the heat of his fires. I sat back and was prepared to watch a man in action but the traitor leaned across the counter and ordered a half of sherry. It was one of the greatest shocks of my life and for a moment I lost faith in the unquenchable spirit of mankind.

People should not be misled by the expression 'he was a great man to drink porter'. I once heard this said about a man as I was returning from his funeral. It does not mean that the man in question was a slave to porter or a phenomenal guzzler of pints. It meant merely that he treated porter with dignity, that he was the best of fellows when under the influence, that he knew when he had enough and, most of all, that he will be missed and sorrowed after, by those who were his drinking companions in moments of plenitude.

And now, if you will excuse me, my corns are at me and I have a touch of neuritis so I'm sure none of you will begrudge me the comfort of a few pints of capably filled porter.

July 1963

Irish Husbands

Isn't it well known that Irish women get the kinds of husband they deserve, what with the mothers plotting and planning from morning till night, advising and coercing them, instead of letting them think for themselves. If a girl is old enough to marry, she's old enough to pick the partner herself; after all 'tis she will have to sleep with him, not the mother.

I've grown weary lately, listening to the litanies of complaints about Irish husbands, who are, in the main, a much-maligned and misunderstood body of agreeable poor fellows. Sure, if the women won't make demands they won't get the results. There's no use in entering a horse for the Grand National if he hasn't been trained to jump and I think you'll agree with me that the course of marriage is as fraught with danger as Aintree.

But there's no use in my making a case for Irish husbands unless I lay before you the evidence to prove my point. A friend of mine, a married woman who has successfully withstood twenty-five years of intimate association with the same man, once told me the following story. He was a great fellow altogether for courting and romancing and crooning, if you don't mind, before they were joined together in holy wedlock. Yerra but man alive after a few years of marriage when the humour was knocked out of him at the rate of a child a year, didn't he turn out to be the most notorious bucko of a blackguard that ever blackened a pair of boots. He was out boozing every night with the boys and off to the dogs every other night while the unfortunate wife stayed at home minding the children.

A friend of hers recommended novenas and another long-suffering martyr gave her a prayer as long as a West Coast come-all-ye. So, she prayed and she prayed that he would come home early and give up his evil ways. But he didn't come home early. He came home late and he didn't come home alone. He brought the boys with him and there was often a case of porter and a couple of naggins of the hot stuff, and that was the cronawning and table-thumping they had all night in the kitchen. Upstairs herself was in bed with the rosary beads entwined around her fingers and she praying away to console herself. Out would come the pan downstairs and out would come the black puddings and the sausages and the chops and when they were full of porter, they ate. Needless to say, they neglected to wash up after them.

Time went by and he landed one night with two other fellows as drunk as himself. Upstairs the rosary beads was put away and she waited till the booze was exhausted and sat up in the bed when she heard his foot on the stairs. He opened the door of the room and turned on the light.

'Come in!' says she; 'come in, you cockeyed son of a bitch,' and with that stinging comment she proceeded to fling the following objects at him:

One rubber hot water bottle from which the stopper had been removed;
One eight-ounce child's feeding bottle;
One four-ounce jar of zinc and castor oil cream;
Two ladies' shoes and one gent's ashtray;
One large wedding photograph;

Two tins of high quality baby powder, one full and one
empty.

Then, finally, she let him have it between the eyes with
(and I use her own words) 'one outsize chamber pot that
would make a hat for an elephant.'

'What was the result?' I asked.

'Ah!' she said, 'that was the meek man and he kneeling
down on the floor begging for forgiveness!'

The final result was that, thereafter, he never went anywhere without her. He saved up and bought a car and a better
father you couldn't find if you travelled a chapel on the last
night of a men's mission.

There is nothing wrong with the average Irish husband
if the wife is willing and able to fight her corner. I'll grant
that you'll find blackguards, but that's the way the world is
made. The average Irishman is a warmer and more generous
person than his continental counterpart. He hasn't half the
plamás or the hair-oil or the roguery but he has twice the
affection. Marriage is a game for two players and there is no
use in appealing to a third party when the going gets rough.

You say 'in France a woman is judged by her intelligence
but in Ireland by her face and figure'.

That's what you think, and I know what I'm talking about
because, after all, I'm one of the many who judge them. The
first thing an Irishman looks for in a woman is common sense.
Next he looks for honesty. The two things he doesn't want
are airs and graces. These he can't stand because he knows
full well they never dressed a bed or darned a sock.

The vast majority of the Irish husbands I know are as
good, if not better, than husbands anywhere in the world.

The women, however, must keep working on them until they are permanently stabilised. It's a game which demands the full participation of both players for the first ten or fifteen years. After that, when he's fully trained, he's a joy to live with.

A goodly number of women have nobody but themselves to blame when their husbands turn out to be blackguards. Before marriage, they harried and hounded the chaps of their choice even when the interest wasn't reciprocated. This is a peculiar kind of obsessive love which has no place in a marriage. If a man doesn't do the chasing, he must be ignored. If he is interested enough he'll be on the ball but when the woman does the chasing she is inviting disaster.

Finally, if there is one thing an Irish husband admires in a wife, it is a bit of genuine temper. He becomes proud of this. In fact, he'll boast about it and he'll often keep his mouth shut because he doesn't want to draw her on him. Yes, indeed, a wife with a good lively temper will never want for a good husband!

Feb 1967

Cold Women

Women are forever complaining about the cold and many I know go to bed in the height of summertime with blistering hot water bottles.

At this time of the year when the sun is on holiday and Jack Frost works overtime, it is not uncommon for a woman to fortify her bed with two and often three hot water bottles and this despite the fact that her sleeping companion may be a husband of great weight and warmth.

This is a time of year, too, when they pretend not to hear the hollering of hungry infants, when they accidentally touch snoring husbands in the back so that he finds himself unaccountably awake and solely responsible for the hunger of his child.

I often wonder what would happen to women if their hot water bottles were taken away; would they sit by the fire all night and forego the comfort of the bed? This is most unlikely in a world where electric blankets are cheaper than women's hats.

I spoke to one woman about electric blankets.

'They're not for me!' she said. 'You can't snuggle them or cuddle them and always there is the terrible thought at the back of your head that you may be in for a bit of a shocker!'

Central heating isn't the answer either because in houses which are adequately heated I have seen as many as six hot water bottles hanging from crooks and nails all over the place and in one country kitchen where a pig was slaughtered only a month before, there were more hot water bottles hanging from the ceiling than flitches of bacon.

Be that as it may, however, this essay is about cold women and not about hot water bottles.

The best cure for a cold woman, if she is single, is to locate a suitable man, marry him and sleep with him. For one thing, she won't need as many hot water bottles and for another she will be mistress of a house where all the hot water bottles are her own.

I am tempted to ask if it is a reflection on a man if his wife is in the habit of going to bed with one or more hot water bottles. It is no such thing because women being what they are it is neither right nor fair, just as a black man's left arm is neither right nor fair, to judge a man on the strength of his wife's idiosyncrasies.

I have been asked, being a man of many experiences, if fat women are warmer than thin women, and vice versa. My own woman is neither fat nor thin and she is as fond of her hot water bottle as the next woman. Some thin women of my acquaintance assure me that they use only one hot water bottle while others, who are twice as fat, use twice as many.

No, all women are just naturally cold when temperatures fall and frost begins to cloud the windows. A chemist of my acquaintance assures me that for every hot water bottle he sells to a man, he sells twenty-three to women. One may reasonably deduce then that women are the colder of the only two known sexes. This must not be held against them. Indeed nature has a good reason for everything. Now, the coldest type of woman is the woman who never opens her mouth. She, I am told by medical friends of some standing, is in danger of freezing. The warmer type of woman is the woman who talks away all day long whether she has an audience or not, but the warmest – the very warmest type of woman is the woman who cuts the daylights out of her neighbours. Every muscle in her body is working when she is going at full stretch. Her excitement increases as she vituperates and when at the top of her form she is so heated that she feels no cold.

I am not saying that women should run their neighbours down as a means of getting warm, not that I have anything against a good bit of needling gossip. In fact, I enjoy listening to it and it would be terrible to deprive women of this fine pastime. The neighbours don't mind as they cannot hear and one may be sure that they are busily engaged in the same pursuit themselves. Husbands enjoy this business more than wives although they would never admit it. They don't actually participate but they nod and hum to show that they are in agreement and often when the conversation flags and when the subject of the criticism is exhaustively dealt with the clever husband will inject the anaemic exchanges with: 'They say she's getting a car of her own!' This is sure to bring sighs and gasps from the women. The flow of blood speeds up thereby warming them so that they forget the nip that is in the air.

In conclusion, I feel that women are at their best when they are cold and beset by whirling winds and frosts. They rise to the occasion. They do not dawdle and are not distracted. Cold weather suits them. It brings a glow to their cheeks and a freshness to their faces and when they hurry briskly through frosty highways they begin to look like girls again.

The Pram

I am not in favour of stylised, streamlined prams.

The glitter of chrome and the polish of plush upholstery do not impress, nor do they make the slightest impression on the inarticulate but happy occupants of lesser prams. Anyway, it is not the pram that matters but the party who is strapped inside.

I am not condemning the gilded conveyance, but the tiny beings who occupy such ornate carriages might not be able to afford such luxury in later years and it might be more profitable to start them off in life without pomp and pretension.

Only a gifted seer should sell a pram because those who part with prams believing that they are no longer wanted will almost always be immediately in need of them again. It is as if God had said: 'I will be the judge of such things!'

Flippant sports prams with drapes and laces are fine for those who can afford a new pram every year but a solid sensible pram will see a sizeable family into the walking stages and even where there is the minimum of time between each arrival the carefully chosen perambulator can comfortably cope with surprising numbers over the years.

A pram is also a good guide to the social aspirations of those who own it although not so much these days since fabulous carriages can be bought for little or nothing on the never-never resulting in the subsequent impoverishment of those who strive for effect.

A glittering pram does not mean that the occupant will be a glittering power in the game of life and a shabby one does not indicate a shabby future for its tenant. No, indeed, for many a great man never sat in a pram at all and huge families have survived the misfortunes of infancy with nothing more than a common go-car.

I have often seen old ladies wheeling pet dogs in expensive prams. There should be a law against this. I have no objection to a dog sitting on a pram if he has a proprietary interest in the welfare of the occupant. I have known old family dogs to fold up and die when the pram was no longer in use. They would sometimes bark and growl at passers-by and I cannot but wholeheartedly approve of these faithful fellows. It is all right to have a look at a new baby but it is not all right to examine the materials of pillow-slips and blankets or to estimate the cost of the baby's garments.

Other legitimate users of prams are newsboys, fruiterers and greengrocers. Where markets move from corner to corner a moveable shop is necessity itself and the retired or bodyless pram is without peer in this respect. Prams are also successfully used for the conveyance of large quantities of bottled stout at Christmas time, and often when promising parties are prematurely ended by the unexpected closure of taverns. Prams have been put to incredible uses, but a recital of these is not necessary, although I remember an old man who used to frequent a certain pub and when he became unsteady after too much drink the family pram was sent for and he was wheeled home ignominiously with his feet hanging out.

Second-hand prams should not be sold unless by second-hand dealers. Prams which are no longer needed should be given away freely whenever possible. If there is such a commodity as good luck, it will certainly follow the giver. I don't know why opulent people should want to hold on to their prams unless it is to remind them of a time when the milk order was at its apex and napkins were the order of the day. When retired prams grow rusty the harmony of a community is endangered and protesting axles scream, not for oil, but for little people with eyes that are full of wonder and legs that kick off the most carefully tucked clothes.

I often ask myself what grandmothers would do if they were deprived of pram-pushing and the opportunity to compare notes about the antics of their inimitable charges. They would sit at home, I suppose, remembering early years of happiness and insolvency when they had prams of their own.

I am told of male pram-pushers. I have not seen them in action and therefore do not know what sort of impression they make. I would not judge them in haste, because no one knows of the prompting circumstances or the problems of the home. Allowing for a normal household, I would not approve of it. It is unseemly and shows a lack of sporting instinct. It could mean a subdued mother sitting wistfully at home. Of course, where the couple walk, the male must take over when inclines arise and I am completely in tune with the father who, when nobody is looking but his wife, pushes the pram at a reckless speed until he is winded, to the delight of both his offspring and himself.

Exercises

A friend of mine recently visited a doctor and complained that he wasn't feeling at all well.

A thorough examination followed, during which the patient took off his shirt and vest to facilitate trial by stethoscope. The doctor, as doctors are wont to do, hummed and hawed a good deal to himself and finally announced that the patient should take up cycling. My friend did so, as instructed, and almost immediately his condition improved. Soon he was back into his old ways, drinking porter and smoking fags. However, he fell from the bicycle while avoiding a car and is presently in hospital nursing a broken ankle. The accident has put him off cycling altogether. He even went so far as to ask me if I would buy the bicycle. When I declined he offered it to me for nothing, but I am not such a fool as to imagine I would survive for long in the saddle if I accepted his generous offer.

Now my friend and I are faced with a serious problem in respect of exercise. Road walking is out of the question. With present mortality rates soaring, the slack-wire is more attractive. Fields have grown soft and mushy and paths are ankle-deep in mud. Woodways are slimy and gummy from the disintegrating corpses of innumerable leaves and one never knows when one will slip and fracture a hip. The dry stubble field is more hazardous that No Man's Land. The air is alive with whining pellets and waspish missiles from the barrels of point twenty-twos. The pedestrian's chances are about the same as the pheasant's.

What is one to do to restrain the puffing paunch and improve the wind? I envy over-coated men with sticks in their hands who instruct misguided heifers in the ways of the road. They can run and jump and dance, and attract no attention. Should I behave in such a fashion there would be little speculation as to my eventual destination. I can hear the neighbours now, cluck-clucking like hatching hens, shaking their heads and whispering: 'We're not at all surprised. We always expected him to crack up sooner or later.'

As I said, paths are muddy and one has to move with extreme caution. For a while, I used to flap my arms violently to exercise the back muscles. I would swing the right around in wide courageous arcs and then the left. Once I took a square inch of skin from the back of my hand after contact with a thorn bush and another time I almost broke my wrist when it came into contact with a tree trunk. However, I persevered, drawing deep whistling draughts of air through my nostrils and ejecting air slowly in text book fashion. As I say, I persevered, until one day a man approached me with a curious expression on his face.

'What do you want?' he asked.

'I'm not with you,' I said. 'Would you kindly explain?'

'I'll explain!' he said. 'You've been signalling me there for the last ten minutes and I've come over a mile to see what was the matter with you.

'I wasn't signalling you!' I protested.

'Yes, you were!' he insisted. 'I was up there ploughing away and minding my own business when you started to wave at me.'

He pointed to a distant hillock over a mile away and there the upturned earth glinted where his plough had furrowed the green surface.

'Sorry!' I said. 'I was just doing a few exercises.'

'How did I know,' he pouted, 'but that it was a stroke you were after getting?'

I apologised and he turned to go but not without a parting shaft: 'Did you ever hear the story of the wolf and the shepherd boy?' he asked.

'Of course!' I answered; 'But where is the analogy?'

'The shepherd boy,' he explained, 'was always cryin the wolf had come and when the neighbours came the no wolf. Finally, the neighbours grew exasperated and the wolf really came, the shepherd roared in vain. You waving in earnest one day, too, and nobody will come to aid.'

With that, he turned on his heel and unhurriedly parted to resume his ploughing. I suspect he was glad of distraction but, on finding that nothing was the matter, g annoyed and decided to take it out on me. I didn't give the hand-fanning immediately, not until several cars stopp to find out why I was waving at them.

There seems, at the moment, to be no way out of th dilemma. At home there isn't enough room for the type of exercise I so desperately need. For a while, I took to throwing stones across the river but sooner or later an audience would gather and one was sure to ask what I was firing at. They refused to believe me when I told them the truth and one day I turned around to find a water-keeper eyeing me suspiciously from behind a bush. I threw him, instead of a stone, a salute but he just stood there with hooded eyes and impassive face. I was forced to move on and eventually compelled to abandon my stone-throwing habits altogether. Then, one day, when I thought nobody was looking, I decided to have a bit of a run on a deserted stretch of roadway. I did several short sprints and got away with them, as I thought, unnoticed.

That night I met a footballer friend in the street. 'I hear you're making a comeback,' he said. 'I'm told you're training on the quiet.'

I was too flabbergasted to reply.

'Keep it up,' he said. 'There's a vacancy for a corner forward in the juniors.'

Paddling

Frost is a friend!

When I say this, I overlook his treatment of early shoots and stalks and apologise for his haphazard glazing of paths and roads.

But friend he is, for he moulds the weather into a compact ring. He gives us the sun and blue skies by day and starry skies at night.

However, I must upbraid him because he puts an end to paddling. He skulks in streams and pools and beaches and demoralises ankles and toes so that they turn blue and black and purple. It is true to say that a man can paddle under any circumstances except frosty ones.

The reason I write about paddling at all is that it would seem to be losing ground in the field of outdoor activities. The dedicated paddler is a cross between a landlubber and a sailor and paddling itself is a pastime which might be described as beneficial and stimulating.

Now, for many years, although not a full-time paddler, I have made a study of paddling and paddlers and I have come to the conclusion that the most enthusiastic and unrelenting of all paddlers is the elderly lady. For a while, I contemplated a short book which I decided to call *The Complete Paddler* or *The Art of Paddling*, but I abandoned the idea as it might have a perverse effect on paddling.

The male paddler is, for the most part, elderly and although toddlers may seem to be more abundant in seaside resorts, he is no more than a splasher and, besides, paddling in a bathing suit is against all the rules.

The senior male paddler is an interesting study. He is quick-tempered and short-winded and he paddles with his neck cocked like a swan as if he were admiring his toes in the water. He begins by taking off his shoes, never his hat. This is followed by removal of socks and, finally, collar and tie. In passing, it might be no harm to mention that it is almost sacrilegious to paddle while wearing a collar and tie. Hats and caps are permissible. Indeed they are the *sine qua non* of all qualified paddlers for while one can easily see the dangers lurking below, one can never be sure of what will come from above. Having removed the aforementioned garments, the male paddler pulls his hat or cap firmly on his head. He rolls up his trousers above the knees, often exhibiting knotty calves and bunion-cluttered feet. He does not care if the purple traceries of his varicose veins attract curiosity. He then places his hands in his trousers' pockets, extends his paunch and saunters seawards. He steps into the water without testing its temperature and savours its salving but at once salt-laden stings. If he were a seal or a dog, he would bark. It would be a deep growl of supreme satisfaction. It is dangerous to disturb him in this, the early stage of his ritual. He bends downwards, grunting like an all-in wrestler, and separates one toe from another until all could be described as having achieved temporary independence.

He then walks in a line parallel with the beach, at a depth of nine inches, looking neither to left nor right. He dislikes noisy swimmers. He does not like to get splashes and may sometimes remonstrate when noisy dippers cross his bows.

When in a semi-bibulous mood he is not above drawing a kick or a clout at those who would encroach upon his preserves.

The elderly female, on the other hand, is a more sedate, more unruffled and a far more happy paddler. She is tolerant of those who occupy the sea and it is conceivable that she may be reciting one of her many novenas as she moves slowly and imperturbably with the ponderous grace of a great sailing ship. The front of her skirt or dress is held in her right hand the way a nervous opera-singer might clutch a silk handkerchief. She smiles at all and sundry, stops to nod at small boys and girls, looks about her betimes to admire the lay of the land and is not above the odd playful kick when she feels that nobody is watching her.

There are, of course, several other kinds of paddlers but the above are the chief ones or what the ornithologist might describe as 'the greater grey-haired wrinkle-crested paddler'.

I have little experience of other types and perhaps am not qualified to investigate them closely and with detachment. One of the earliest paddles I remember was conducted by a female relation of my mother's. I was very small at the time and we were walking along the beach hand in hand minding our own business. She was about twenty at the time and she was the first to notice that a man was following us. She said it as if she disapproved but from her face, one might safely gather that she was markedly excited. He passed us back and forth several times after that and endeavoured to attract her attention with a variety of salutes and grimaces of which any actor might be proud. Finally, he approached and asked if she would care for a paddle. He wasn't a bad-looking chap.

'All right!' she said, 'but you'll have to take the child by the hand.'

I dared to presume that they were not unacquainted.

The ultimate upshot of the paddle was that now the pair are happily married with a large family.

Awkward Salutations

The wrong kind of salutation can irritate the recipient and one should be careful when approaching a likely candidate for a salute.

It's all right with people you know and with people you don't know. The trouble arises with people you only half-know.

For instance, if there is a bank manager with whom you have a nodding acquaintance, and whose name is John, coming along the street, it is not wise to say 'How's Jack?' He might not like it. It might be all right for other bank managers and people who have no overdrafts but the ordinary individual would be well advised to say 'Good day, Mr Whatever-his-name-is'.

'Mr' is always safe, unless you use it on a chap you know well. He may think you're being sarcastic and if he's short-tempered might be provoked to draw a wallop at you.

I remember well coming out of a football match in Tralee with two friends some years ago. As we walked down the street a medium-sized thin man, going slightly bald, approached.

'Good evening!' he said, as we passed.

'Good evening, Fred!' one of my friends said.

The medium-sized man stopped in his tracks and asked: 'Are you trying to be funny, sonny?'

'No, no,' said my friend. 'I thought you were Fred Astaire, as God is my judge!'

At this, the stranger lost patience and, if we hadn't intervened, there would have been blows. We parted amicably enough despite the fact that a fair-sized crowd had gathered.

As we moved down the street, a little shaken from the encounter, a man dressed in clerical garb approached.

'Nice evening, father!' we said.

He acknowledged the salute with a wave of his hand. However, our friend who had earlier mistakenly called the man Fred, did not salute at all.

'That's a nice thing!' we reproached him. 'You passed a priest without saluting him.'

'Look!' he explained, 'I didn't know whether he was a priest or a Christian Brother and I'm not taking any more chances.'

We proceeded apace until we came to the door of a tavern well known to us. As we were about to enter, a stout man, wearing a cap, passed by on a bicycle.

'How's Arthur?' our friend shouted for devilment, and we quickly disappeared into the tavern. Inside, while we waited for our drinks to be filled, we noticed that the man on the bicycle had followed us in. Our friend who had addressed him as Arthur did his best to conceal himself behind a bar stool. To no avail, however, because Arthur approached and shook him by the hand.

'I feel very put out,' Arthur said, 'that you should know me and I not know you.'

'That's all right,' our friend said. 'My own memory isn't the best sometimes.'

'Still,' said Arthur, 'you might take it to be bad manners on my part if I passed you without saying "hello!" to you.'

With that, he paid for our drinks and called for one himself. We spent a pleasant half-hour in conversation. Arthur, it transpired, was a stranger to the town and was delighted that someone knew him by name. If his name had not been Arthur and had been, for instance, Algernon or Eric, we would have been involved in another argument.

For me, the most difficult time used to be when I was approached by two men, one of whom was not on speaking terms with me. The thing to do, of course, is to say: 'Turning a bit soft,' or 'Will it last?' This way the situation is nicely covered, but what does one do when one is approached by a single person with whom one is not on speaking terms?

One can, of course, cross the road but that would be an admission of defeat. One can turn around and go back the way one came. This is the sensible thing to do, provided you look up at the sky, giving the impression that in your opinion it's going to rain and that you are doing the right thing by wanting to turn back.

When I was younger and seriously taking notice of girls for the first time, there was a tendency to hurry past girls you would really like to salute. It was a mixture of cowardice and shyness. For this reason it was advisable to bring along a younger soul and to put him up to saluting the girl in question. If she saluted back, which she invariably did, she not only saluted the innocent youth but the person in his company as well.

Meeting mothers of girls was another serious problem. You couldn't very well say: 'Hello, missus!' or she might think you were forward. You couldn't be too effusive, either, or she might think you were only saluting her on account of her daughter. People like to be saluted for their own sakes. I know I do.

But, where was I?

Yes! People who drive motor cars have an edge on other saluters. They don't have to know names or faces. All they have to do is raise the left hand from the steering wheel without looking to right or left and the job is done. Saluting them back is difficult because they are generally too far away by the time one is ready to return the salute. They take it for granted that the salute will be acknowledged, so it is not really necessary to salute them back.

Salute, always salute and be damned, is the best policy. You may not get as many back as you give but you'll also get ones you never expected in the first place.

Tasty Dressers

There are only a few tasty dressers to be seen in this atomic age. Carelessness is the fashion.

I once had an uncle, who was somewhat odd I will admit. On Sunday mornings, he spent from forty to forty-five minutes polishing his shoes before setting out for Mass. Even then he might not be quite satisfied because he was quite capable of turning back at the door to spend another five minutes brushing a smudged upper or a dusty heel.

Look about you at this present time and you'll find that shiny shoes are the exception rather than the rule. Today's young man is content to pull a pullover over his head and shine his shoes against the backs of his trouser legs. In my youth every young man had his own box of polish and his own brushes – one for polishing and one for shining. The truly fastidious would have a square foot of chamois as well. This was used to bring out the very last glint in toe-cap and upper.

The few who pay attention to dress these days are for the most part ex-army men. These are always nattily rigged out and their shoes are always polished. You can easily recognise them by their brown footwear. If the army did nothing else for them, it taught them to look after their appearance.

A word of advice to those faced with interviews for positions. Find out first if the interviewer is an army man. If so, buy a pair of strong brown shoes and shine them till the leather is hot. Wear a tie, not a gaudy one, preferably a grey or a green. Let your suit be conservative in colour and, above all, invest in a close haircut the day before. If you doubt me, let me put it to this way. Let us say, for argument's sake, there are two other candidates for the position, one with a beard, black trousers and a pullover, the other with long hair, embroidered shirt and pixie-type shoes. I ask you, what chance have they got against you?

Years ago, when I was seven or eight, I used to spend my summer holidays in the country. On Sunday evenings when the cows were milked the supper would be quickly eaten and the young men of the household would cast anxious glances at the clock on the mantelpiece. The time would be six o'clock, as a rule. The starting time of the dance that night would be nine o'clock. This left three hours. Each of the young men in turn would press his good trousers and hang it over a chair near the fire to dry out. The next hour would be spent in an unmerciful washing, scrubbing and scraping of the entire anatomy so that skins were a bristling pink. Then came the shoes. They would be wiped off first with a damp cloth and then with a dry cloth. Then came the polish, sparingly but evenly, and finally came the shining. This was all done, by the way in vest and trousers without hurry and with obvious relish. Looking back on it now, I believe that the preparations were more enjoyable than the dance itself. All these young men are now married themselves and I wonder what their thoughts are like when they watch their own sons getting ready.

When the shoes were shone, it was time to shave and this took at least another half an hour. No hair, no matter how small, from the base of both ears to the Adam's apple was overlooked and just to make sure they shaved themselves a second time with the mirror at a different angle because the light was tricky and hasty shaving often left a tuft like a triopal.

Nails were then scrubbed and hands washed immaculately clean. The man of the house generally went out to walk the land while these operations were in progress. It would be an embarrassment to both parties if he remained. The mother, like a boarding-school matron, was constantly on call. If it wasn't a lost cuff-link, it was a missing tie. Unerringly she located the missing accessories, although hers was strictly the sock, shirt and vest department. These she laid out on the big table at the appropriate time. Around half-eight, there was an air of bustle and excitement. Vests and shirts were donned first. The trousers were pulled on carefully to protect the razor-like creases. Then came the socks and shoes and the coat. Funnily enough, the tie was always left till last, as country folk wear ties as little as possible while indoors.

Now all were dressed and everything was set but the mother insisted on making a final check. They submitted to this with groans and banter although they really didn't mind it at all. Then they checked themselves and one, the crackedest and youngest, danced a few impatient steps on the floor, mad to be off. Looking back on them now – they glowed with cleanliness and good health.

There would be another on-the-spot cleaning when they had parked their bikes in the town. This was carried out with handkerchiefs and fistfuls of dock-leaves or grass.

Alas, those tasty dressers are no more. The pace is too fast and there are too many young men in a hurry going nowhere.

I look around, in vain, these days for a dapper young man, but he is nowhere to be seen. Maybe it is because there is no attention to detail, to the smaller, finer things which really count in the last analysis. Whatever it is, there is a void because there was always something admirable and refreshing about a tasty dresser.

Sneezing

Whenever I look at the sun, I sneeze.

This I because the sun has certain sternutatory properties which are some of the principal sources of all sneezes, great and small.

I am no lover of small sneezes. Indeed, I find them frustrating and unnerving and sometimes they can leave me in a state of abject depression for several minutes. The large or full sneeze, on the other hand, is a satisfying and somewhat enjoyable sensation. Worst of all is the unborn or stifled sneeze, the practice of which is detrimental to good humour. A mature sneeze, which has been carefully manufactured in the sneeze-box, should not be stifled. It may be staggered into a succession of smaller sneezes. This is a common practice and there are nervous people who favour staggered sneezes in case they get their heads blown off or burst a blood-vessel with one explosive sneeze.

In every community, civilised or otherwise, there is always an outstanding sneezer. I will call these people born sneezers because they can sneeze at the drop of a hat and once they start there is no stopping them. They go on and on and just when you think they've exhausted all supplies they unexpectedly continue with a sustained barrage, until their faces are a glowing red and their eyes swimming in water. The born sneezer will sneeze anywhere and there's no point in trying to stop him. In fact, it is extremely dangerous to interfere.

I know, personally, of an interesting case in this respect. A friend of mine, now working as a cocktail barman in Montreal, was a born sneezer. He enjoyed sneezing and when in the company of trusted friends he would place a hand on the shoulder of the nearest one to get purchase in order to sneeze all the more effectively. Once, in a strange town, he was in the middle of a fit of sneezing, when a man came up behind him and gave him a hearty slap on the back. It had no effect on the sneezing, so another even heartier slap was administered. My friend caught hold of the backslapper's hand and continued to sneeze. He was at this stage completely absorbed in the sneezing so he could not tell the backslapper to go away. He held on to him until he could sneeze no more and when he had finished he hauled out and let the backslapper have it on the solar plexus. Litigation followed, but as things turned out, the case was settled amicably out of court and there was no more about it.

The incident, however, served a twofold purpose. It taught our friend the sneezer that, during future sneeze orgies, he should keep his back to the wall and it taught the backslapper, well-meaning though he was, that to interrupt a born sneezer was as dangerous as baiting a water-buffalo. I'm sure that he gave all sneezers a wide berth thereafter.

What of sneezing as a means of communication? It is as important and effective as any other. I, myself, have found this to be true in the streets of major cities and, indeed, on lonely country roads. As I explained earlier, whenever the sun shines bright I am inclined to sneeze, not continuously but a good sun is worth at least two good sneezes and possibly one minor. Complete strangers have stopped and said: 'God bless you!' then smiled and passed on about their business. Whenever I hear a man sneeze, I bless him too, although I may never have seen him before in my life. I am disappointed when there is nobody around to bless me after a sneeze. I do not find the same satisfaction in sneezing and there is an empty feeling which persists for quite a while.

A friend of mine assures me that the following story is true. It concerns a second cousin of his who was an assistant cook in the navy, a shy reticent man who found it difficult to communicate with people. He had been jilted by three sweethearts because of this reticence and this despite the fact that he neither drank nor smoked, had money in the post office, and was a certainty to be a master cook in due course. About once every three years he got a fit of sustained sneezing which persisted for several minutes.

Then one day while walking down a city street, during his furlough, he was suddenly assailed by a fit of uncontrollable sneezing. He stopped when he found it coming on because none, but the unwise, sneeze while walking. He started and by the time he had reached the third sneeze, he heard somebody say: 'God bless you!' Through his mist-filled eyes, he discerned a tall girl wearing an off-white coat and a headscarf. She had been cycling past to buy sausages for her brother's supper and felt compelled to dismount since there was nobody around to bless our friend the cook after he had sneezed. She stood there patiently and every time the cook sneezed she said 'God bless you!' He concluded with a record-breaking feat of thirty-two sneezes so that the girl was there for quite a while and it could be said that they got to know each other during the sneezing. He thanked the girl profusely and a short polite conversation followed during which he made a date for the pictures. They were married within the space of three months and a happier couple you couldn't find anywhere. Whenever he gets a fit of sneezing they both laugh and remember the time when they first met and fondly recollect that it was a fit of sneezing which brought them to-gether.

Eaves-shoots

The other day I watched, spellbound, while a stout, middle-aged man eviscerated an eaves-shoot from the top of a thirty-foot ladder.

Beneath him, another man, younger and less energetic, held the ladder steady. He did this by placing his right leg on the lowest rung and his two hands on the fifth.

The man at the top scooped out a fistful of earth and grass and let it plop to the ground where it spread itself out like a pancake. The man holding the ladder seemed oblivious to the life around him. He rested his jaw on the fifth rung while his body hung slack. He stared through the rungs like a lifer who has been unjustly convicted. Above him, the shoot-cleaner stretched precariously to the extremes of his arc and sometimes he, too, paused to look down and around. He was not looking for diversion.

In his wisdom, he took time off to measure the distance between himself and the ground. He reminded me of a careful ship's navigator who, finding himself in unchartered waters, plots assiduously and frequently lest his vessel veer into disaster. After a while he climbed down, stopping after every seventh or eighth step, sometimes to adjust his cap, other times to hitch up his trousers and once to pick his teeth with his index finger.

On the ground, he spoke to his assistant and, between them, they shifted the ladder to another part of the house-front. They smoked cigarettes leisurely and conspired in whispers. Then he climbed the ladder again and resumed where he had left off.

Beneath him, the ladder-holder became engaged in a conversation with a passer-by, heedless of the plopping silt which spattered on the street and roadway.

Down the street, two girls tripped, the noise of their high heels like revolver-shots. One went under the ladder but the other skirted it. The girl who went under the ladder smiled at the young man who was holding it.

'You're very serious!' she quipped.

To this he made no reply but when the girls joined forces again, he leered after them and emitted a long unmelodious whistle. The ladder trembled and shifted and the man at the top held on grimly. Quickly he took in what had happened and with a judicious fistful of high quality mud reminded his assistant where his first duties lay.

Duly the shoots were cleaned and the ladder was laid flat on the roadway. The older man knocked at the door of the house to claim his wages. A woman emerged, opened her purse and handed him three half-crowns.

'God grant you a silver bed in heaven,' he thanked her and handed a half-crown to the younger man.

The next house was mine. At the time, I happened to be standing in the doorway.

'Do you want your shoots cleaned?' the older man asked.

'Not today!' I told him, 'maybe tomorrow. You see, I'm just going out.'

'We won't have the ladder tomorrow,' the young man interjected. 'We have only the loan of it for today.'

'All right,' I said. 'How much?'

'Ten bob,' they both said.

'You only charged the woman next door seven-and-six,' I reminded them.

'Quite so,' said the older man, 'but hers was done last year and yours wasn't done for three.'

'My house is lower,' I said, for the sake of argument.

"Tis lower,' said the assistant, 'but 'tis wider.'

'All right!' I conceded. 'Go ahead.'

Without hurry, the ladder was shortened and arranged against the wall. 'Do you do many a day?' I said to the assistant.

'Yours is the seventh,' he replied.

'Many ten bob ones?' I asked.

He made a mental calculation. 'Four,' he answered smugly. 'Then there was a brace at seven-and-six and one at fifteen bob.'

'Do you get a fixed percentage of the take?' I asked.

'No,' he answered. "Tis all the same to me if 'twas a palace he was doing. I still get a half-crown.'

'He's doing nicely out of it,' I said, indicating the man at the top.

'He is,' said the assistant, 'but his nerves is gone, even though he don't show it.' He looked up-road and seemed to go deeper into thought.

'Do you see me?' he said, in a conspiratorial tone.

'I do,' I said.

'Well,' he continued, 'I'm as hard a man as you would be likely to meet but I wouldn't go up that ladder for a million.'

'Why not?'

'I'll tell you why not,' he said and he tipped his forehead.

'Claustrophobia is why not and that's no cowboy story.'

Soon the silt of my eaves-shoots began to plop merrily to the pavement. 'You could set spuds up here,' the man at the top called, but it was plain he was only trying to justify the charge of ten shillings.

Down the other side of the street came a girl in her teens.

'How's Kate?' the assistant called and he waved a hand at her. Again the ladder trembled. Kate waved back and continued on her way. 'Nice cut of a girl!' the assistant said, half to himself.

Down the ladder came his superior. There was pain on his face.

'What have you against me?' he demanded of his assistant. 'That's the second time today you tried to do me in. Is there nothin' but girls in your head?'

Having said this, the superior climbed the ladder again, followed by a surly look from the assistant. Eventually my shoots were cleaned and I handed over the ten shillings.

'May every hair on your head turn into a candle,' said the superior, 'and light your way to heaven.'

Childminding

I have a theory about minding children and that is – mind them yourself or be without them.

It is as difficult to follow the course of a small boy's movements as it is to track a rampaging satellite and it is only the fact that he is one's own that makes it a bearable pursuit. I have more than an academic interest in the behaviour of small boys when in the company of adults and here are a few unknown facts which should provide the reader with some insight.

In ninety-nine cases out of a hundred when a man has one of his own children and somebody else's child in his charge he will, subconsciously or consciously, pay more attention to his own and this despite the fact that he may have contracted to guarantee equal rights to both.

A relation of mine once asked if he could take one of my kids to the seaside and I readily concurred. Away they went, a light-hearted happy bank, his own kids delighted with the newcomer and the newcomer equally delighted with the prospect of sea and sand.

At six o'clock that evening the 'phone rang and a garda sergeant informed me that he had a child of mine in his custody. My heart nearly stopped and I hurried to collect the lost one.

Later I met the man in whose charge he had been. He was the epitome of apology.

'Isn't it funny,' I said, 'that it wasn't one of your own you lost?'

'By Gobs,' he agreed, 'now that I come to think of it, 'tis funny all right!'

Once, in the city, some years ago, I was given complete charge of a small boy while his parents took a few hours well-deserved rest. We decided to go to the pictures. The picture wasn't very interesting, so he asked to be taken to the toilet. He paid nine other visits in the space of an hour but that wasn't too bad because it was when our time came to leave our bus that he adamantly refused to do so.

'You'll have to get off here,' I explained.

'I can't wait any longer!' the bus conductor shouted.

'Haven't you any kids of your own?' I asked.

'Oh, sure!' he said, 'but they're not like that little brat.'

My friend and I resented this. 'Hit him a wallop!' he urged.

'I'd like to see you try,' the conductor said.

'Go on!' said my small friend.

'Come on!' said the conductor and he took off his bag.

'What's up, Tom?' the driver called.

'Chap here threatening to beat me up!' said the conductor.

The bus driver left his cab and entered the bus.

'Pick on someone your own size!' he said.

I tried to explain as best I could and finally seized the small disturber in my arms. He kicked a lot and shouted but I succeeded. As I alighted from the bus, the conductor kicked me in the behind. I put down the young fellow, but the bus had gone.

Years ago, too, when I was younger and less wise I was in the habit of saying: 'Go on out and enjoy yourselves and I'll look after them.' A man who makes a statement of this kind should have his head examined.

Once I was put in charge of four nephews. At nine o'clock the house was as quiet as a graveyard. Then, when they were absolutely certain that the parents had made good their escape, they started their campaign. It began with the sound of muffled pattering feet. This I ignored because it may have been a genuine visit to the toilet but when, after a while, a piece of mortar fell from the ceiling, I decided it was time to investigate.

They had uprooted the floorboards and one of the four was missing.

'Come out of there!' I shouted.

He emerged from under the floorboards. 'There was a rat eating us,' he explained.

I replaced the floorboards and restored order. They started again shortly afterwards. A strong trickle of water came down the side of the wall and I rushed to investigate. All the upstairs taps were on and the stoppers were stuck glutinously in the holes of the bath and sinks. I had permission to administer physical punishment if their crimes warranted it but while it is all very fine to slap one's own children on the behind, it is a breach of the peace to do it to others. I decided to stay upstairs where I quickly became exhausted and fell asleep.

Over the years, however, I have acquired considerable know-how in the art of childminding. Its most important aspect is that it's a chore which can never be taken lightly, even by the full-time professional. A woman of my acquaintance told me of the following method: when at the seaside or in a hotel or on the train one of her children creates disorder or causes damage, she pretends she doesn't own the child at all. She is as quick to condemn his capers as anybody else.

'Somebody,' she said, 'is bound to get tired of it and by waiting patiently the child will be subdued and/or reprimanded by others.'

I have been attacked by cross children and I apply the same stratagem as I do with cross dogs. I close my eyes and sit perfectly still and when I open my eyes again I find they have gone away. The slightest awareness of the attacker or the slightest reaction is the first step on the road to disaster.

However, having said all that, I am fond of children with a bit of crossness in them.

Confessions of a Golf-clown

When I was a garsún, all golfers were swells and swanky people, who wore plus-fours and who belonged to another world.

A lot of people felt as I did and the late Jimmy O'Dea, who knew his audiences like the back of his hand, was the most indulgent of entertainers. I can see him now, as Mrs Mulligan, on the stage of the Royal. The phone rings and a posh voice is heard to ask: 'Is Anastasia inside?'

'No,' says Mrs Mulligan in a posher voice, 'she's out with Louis playing golluf.'

But progress is a most reliable leveller and now everybody plays golf – or tries to play it. I even played it myself and still occasionally try to do so but since the man who was my instructor suffered a nervous breakdown, as a result I am now forced to rely for guidance on gentlemen who are avoided by respectable golfers.

I daresay I could be described as a golf-clown, that is to say I look like a golfer and act like a golfer but fail to perform like a golfer.

I can talk like a golfer, too, and in this respect I have few equals. I have, if I may say so, an interesting turn of phrase. I can unite three or four simple expletives into a single sentence which would make a caddy blush. No mean feat this, because there are golfers who believe that caddies cannot blush.

You should see me stretched on a green eyeing the hole down the length of my putter. Visiting enthusiasts who did not know about me would stop and momentarily forget their own game just to watch me. I knew I looked good. I would put on my Bogart leer and switch, as I rose to study the conditions of the green, to my Steiger stare. I used to stall, hoping the onlookers would go away. I would dry my sweat-free hands against the seat of my pants and dry the handle of the putter under my armpit but still I was under observation. Finally, in exasperation, I would putt and, having putted, would putt again. By the time the onlookers would have their backs turned to me and I knew by the agitation of their shoulders that they were smothering laughter.

The man who was my partner would shake his head in admiration when I holed after three putts.

'I'll say one thing for you,' he would console me, 'you're the most consistent golfer I know and I've known them all. Some hole in one putt, some in two, but you never fail to hole in three.'

Of late, I am more of a spectator than a golfer. If I'm away from home and there's a tourney on television I will locate a lounge where there is a set. There are always a few other viewers there before me and while we wait for the viewing to commence, we take stock of each other. Finally, one asks: 'Do you play yourself, sir?'

To this I merely nod and look away as if I were being bored. A poor golfer, on an occasion like this, would hold forth on the more colourful moments of this career but I am of the belief that a scratch golfer would just nod. So I nod and pretend that I am a scratch golfer. While the play progresses on the screen the other viewers look at me now and then as if they would consult me but my mien mesmerises them for they are all handicapped.

Do not for a moment get the impression that I am a theoretical golfer. The truth is, I like to link theory with practice. I play my best golf in public houses where my audience is composed of men whose drinks I have bought for them. If somebody asks me 'What did you go around in yesterday?' I answer 'I went round in an hour and a half which is a course record!'

June 1967

Travellers' Tales

You can fool some of the people all of the time.

Of that there can be no doubt. There are certain women of my acquaintance who believe almost everything they are told and who then proceed to act accordingly. They are, if I might be permitted the use of an American word, suckers for a good story. As the tale of misfortune unfolds, their eyes begin to moisten and feverishly they search pockets for a purse to find succour for the distraught storyteller.

I, myself, like a good story and while I may not believe a word of it, I pay according to quality. I do not believe in payment per thousand words. I like a high standard and, regardless of length, once the bones are there, I cough up without regret.

For instance, recently in Limerick city, where I went to see a film, I met an excellent storyteller. Our car was parked in that part which nestles near the river, overlooking the falls of Curraghour.

We were on our way from the cinema, a friend and I, accompanied by our two wives, when we were accosted by a shawled woman who asked for help. She had a good face and she made the most of the short time at her disposal. Her opening gambit was a blessing of singular beauty: 'May God straighten the road for ye!' This was at once a reflection on county councils everywhere who are slow about straightening roads and at the same time a tribute to the Almighty for whom straightening roads is a formality if He were so inclined. We – the menfolk – contributed to the woman's up-keep and went on our way but our womenfolk remained behind listening enraptured to a story which the shawled woman unfolded for them.

We stood by the car waiting. My friend lit a cigarette while we admired the fine full moon which shed a languorous light on the Shannon river.

We were approached by a small battle-scarred man with a face as hard as nails and a week's beard bristling on his jaw.

'Would you oblige me with a fag?' he said.

My friend handed him a cigarette and he then asked to be provided with a light. He thanked us profusely and went away. But he only went a little bit. The request for the cigarette was his method of gauging our defences for it is widely known that if a man does not refuse you for a cigarette, he may not refuse you for financial assistance.

He returned and stood before us shamefacedly with his eyes fixed on the cigarette which still glowed between his fingers. The ends of his trousers were frayed and his elbows thrust themselves indecently through the sleeves of his coat.

'I hate to ask,' he said, 'but I want a few bob desperately!'

'For what?' I asked, knowing that he was in need of a cure.

'The wife is in hospital and I'm left with nine kids,' he said. 'All I want is the price of a few loaves of bread.'

I'm sure he had intended asking for the price of one loaf but he notice the sympathetic look on our faces and decided to ask us for the price of two.

'What's the matter with the wife?' my friend asked.

This knocked the man off his trot for a second but only for a second.

'They took her in,' he said, 'to take out her appendix.'

'Who's minding the children?' I asked.

'No one,' he said, 'but the eldest has a bit of sense and she'll keep them in some sort of order till I get the bread.'

'Why don't you get a job?' my friend asked.

'Can't work!' he replied. 'I have ulsters in my stomach and one of the hands is paralysed.'

We cluck-clucked with deep sympathy.

''Tis not for myself,' he said; ''tis for the kids!'

He had a nice way of making a point and a nice tight way of expressing himself. He shifted continuously from one foot to the other, not because one foot was more tired that the other but because he wanted us to see the broken shoes he was wearing. He could not have been more eloquent, not even if he had pointed at them.

We gave him a few shillings and he thanked us in a most gracious fashion. Then, quicker that the eye could see, he topped the cigarette, pocketed the money and sped like a hare to a car which had just parked and from which an elderly man with a kind face and horn-rimmed spectacles was alighting. The elderly man listened for a while, then put his hand on the man's shoulder as if to console him. The elderly man then searched his pockets and parted with his change as if it was he who was being favoured. Meanwhile our two women had successfully broken away from the shawled woman. They came towards the car slowly. One was dabbing her eyes with a handkerchief. The other was blowing her nose. Around the eyes of both were the stains of recent tears. We opened the car doors and ordered them into their seats where they sat silently, sniffing faintly, while the engine was being started.

'That poor woman!' said one.

'God help her!' said the other.

'She has an awful cross!' said one.

'Desperate!' said the other.

'Do we thank God half enough?' said one.

'We should be down on our knees all day,' said the other.

We, the menfolk, remained respectfully silent while they told us how the woman's husband was in hospital undergoing a serious operation from which he might not recover.

'I gave her ten bob,' said one wife.

'So did I!' said the other.

The car was started and as we turned towards home we beheld the man who had recently touched us. He was huddled with the shawled woman under a Guinness sign. They appeared to be counting their pooled money and they looked – although the light was deceptive – to be a very contented couple.

April 1967

Horoscopes

Lately, out of curiosity, I started to read my horoscope.

There is one magazine, in particular, which always provides a highly coloured account of the shape of things to come.

Last month, a long journey was predicted. There was to be an improvement in my financial status and a joyous reunion with a long-lost friend.

Strangely enough, there was a certain amount of truth in the forecast, although not in the precise way that I expected.

First of all, there was the long journey and, as things turned out, it was not only long, it was also arduous. Hitch-hiking to Limerick, I had to walk three miles of the way before being picked up by the obliging driver of an ice-cream van.

The improvement in my financial status came when I found a sixpenny bit and two halfpence in the pocket of an old trousers.

Lastly, there was the joyful reunion with the old friend. This, too, came true. I met him in O'Connell Street in Dublin and he tapped me for a fiver. It was indeed a joyful reunion ... for him!

I have often tried to imagine what the feelings of a ninety-year-old woman must be when she reads a horoscope like this:

> *Danger lies in swimming and mountain climbing in the early part of the month. You would be well advised to turn down a coming proposal of marriage from a much older person. There is romance and the promise of a lasting friendship towards the end of the month. Beware of conflict in the home, especially with your parents.*

I have never read of a ninety-year-old woman addicted to swimming or mountain climbing, although there may be exceptions, but it is the romance and the promise of the lasting friendship which intrigue me. The conflict with parents does not promise to be lively since both would be around the 120-years age group.

My idea of a sensible horoscope would be something like this:

> *Do not touch exposed electric wires or jump into deep holes if you cannot swim. Do not jump out of an aeroplane without a parachute or you will come to grief. Your financial status will improve if you stop drinking and smoking.*

Alas, the only thing predictable about this life is that it will come to an end, for everybody, sooner or later, but what is one to believe if the horoscope unexpectedly predicts a sudden change of climate? Can this mean a hasty departure from this world to the next, or does it merely mean sunburn and bathing-togs?

On another occasion, my horoscope predicted:

Your luck and love of life usually improve at this time of year and it would be a wise time to get married. Meanwhile problems in the home could mount to an unprecedented degree causing you to move out or to make rearrangements of some kind.

There was a lot of truth in the latter part of this prediction. Maybe it was a good time to get married but since I was already married, I had no way of knowing. Certainly a proposal to my wife regarding a second marriage would result in my having to move on, or, as the horoscope prophesied, to make rearrangements of some kind.

Last month, I looked at my wife's horoscope and saw that 'past confusions were now cleared away. Do not worry about taking direct action where partnership money is involved and, above all, do not worry what others think.'

Being the only other partner in the firm I was a little concerned so I read the horoscope for her. Then I decided to hold a watching brief and to say nothing. Towards the end of the prescribed period I noticed a sudden change. The advent of new curtains started it off. Next came wallpaper and paint and threats about the purchase of new blankets. A portable radio was purchased and there was talk of carpets. Luckily, the horoscope for the following week advised caution in monetary matters. Heaven knows where it would have ended but for that.

I am a Gemini man myself and at the moment my spirits should tend to be raised and my output steady ... or so the horoscope says. Nothing could be further from the truth. I have a pain in the tooth, a scurrilous and most unwelcome corn and my output was never worse. My input is disastrous, however, because I am afflicted with unpredictable attacks of heartburn. I would very much like to meet the party who was responsible for my horoscope and ask him where his cock-suredness comes from.

The moral of this little treatise is that the future is best left in the hands of the Creator, not to some swarthy señorita with dangling earrings and monstrous bangles. Anybody who takes a horoscope seriously is in for a succession of suck-ins. You can push the Himalayas with the right machinery but you cannot push luck and all the money in the world cannot purchase a glimpse into what lies around the corner.

Pigs' Heads

Earth has not anything to show more fair:
Dull would be he of soul who could pass by
A sight so touching in its majesty.

WORDSWORTH

Life is funny and life is short, but life would be a lot funnier if it were and longer, and life, I very much fear, with the good things in it, is not availed of fully, and the tragedy is that people pass on to the next life without tasting the true pleasures of this one.

To illustrate my point, let me tell the story of the jackdaw and the sparrow. It was Christmas and the river was frozen over. The jackdaw tried vainly to break the ice with his beak. He was thirsty but the ice was thick, and, knock as he would, the ice remained firm. A sparrow arrived on the scene and studied the jackdaw cautiously for a while.

'Any hope of a drink?' he asked, when he saw that the jackdaw meant him no harm.

'Nothing doing!' said the jackdaw. 'I've been knocking here for half an hour, and no answer so far.'

'Hard lines!' mused the sparrow. 'I'm piping with the thirst.'

'I could do with a drink myself,' said the jackdaw.

'Ah!' said the sparrow, 'we didn't drink it while we had it!'

The moral of this story is that men die without even once having tasted pig's head. They might have done so if

they had bothered to pace themselves in the race of
cupidity and lack of insight disabled their facultie
prived them of proper judgement when it came down to
portant things.

I have little admiration for men who make millions, but
I have respect for a man who shows restraint when he is
faced with a plate of pig's head and cabbage and I don't care
what others may think, but for me a pig's head exhibited in
a window has as winning a way with it as a platter of engage-
ment rings or a regiment of chops.

Hot or cold, the pig's head is a man's food. Put him with
any company you like – kale, cabbage or turnips – and he
will hold his own because, like all true nobility, he can mix
with king or commoner. To those who view him for the first
time, his appearance may be against him, but to close one's
eyes and savour the first unforgettable mouthful is an experience which nobody should forego and indeed, if house-
wives had any sense of justice, no child should be permitted
to reach the use of reason without having first tasted pig's
cheek.

If I were a prospective employer and I were interviewing
a man for a position of trust, I would not fall into the trap of
asking him the usual unrevealing questions, such as where he
went to school and the extent of his past experience in relation to the job. There is no more reliable guide in the assess-
ment of a man's character than to ask him bluntly what his
opinions are with regard to pig's head. If he frowns and shakes
his head, the interview should be terminated there and then,
but if he smiles and tells you there is nothing in the world
like it, you have a man who will not only meet the require-

ments of the job but who will enhance the position by filling it, a man who loves his mother, and is not ashamed of his poor relations – in short, a man of breeding and discernment.

The pig's head is equally suited to large families and small families. For the large families a whole pig's head provides a satisfying, digestible meal so that when the time has come for vacating the table, there are no cries of complaint. For the small family, the remains of the meal may be put aside until nightfall. A safe place of concealment should be the primary concern because neighbours, regardless of their honesty, are, after all, only human. One pick counsels another and the next thing you know there is an empty plate, and when the man of the house returns after his few pints of porter and goes to the press for his piece of pig's head only a hardhearted cynic could remain unmoved at the tragic expression of disappointment on his face.

For the development of neck muscles in children, the bone is recommended. It strengthens teeth and, although many may disagree with me, early enthusiasm for the jawbone has resulted in some excellent public house singers. If during the meal the conversation revolves around weighty issues, a man may chew the pig's tongue and cogitate with advantage. If he wants to drive home an observation, all he has to do to attract attention is to stick his fork into a sliver of lean meat and hold it aloft while he speaks.

Resentment becomes no man, but resentment is unavoidable when one listens to cheap music hall comments which endeavour to bracket the pig's head with louts and buffoons. Again resentment rises when we hear of the denials of our boys and girls who leave to work in the cities. All their lives they have known pigs' heads, eaten pigs' heads and relished pigs' heads but fear of ridicule makes them ashamed to mention pigs' heads, and when the pig's head is drawn down derogatively they laugh with the rest as if they were above such vulgar indulgence, as if they had never been sent shopping by hard-working mothers, well instructed in the choosing of white-hearted cabbage and well versed in the characteristics of the better-class half-head.

One can understand when young people deny the townland of their upbringing and sing no longer of the hills of home, but there is no excuse for those who deny pig's head and cabbage. They are destined to live empty lives of pretence and destined to occupy the positions of underlings regardless of the reward and responsibilities of their positions for a man who is ashamed of the simple pleasures of the past is neither a dreamer nor a builder. He is party to fraud because he will not be himself and he is easily led because betrayal and surrender are second nature to him.

On the other hand there is hope for the nation while we have young men who still insist on the old classic courses for dinner, young men who will not be easily duped or influenced, young men who will have no hesitation in resorting to physical redress at the least delineation of subjects which they have been reared to respect.

They need have no fear of defeat because pig's head is a bone-builder and a muscle-giver, and a man after a meal of chicken and bread-stuffing is at the mercy of the man who has dined on pig's head.

Sept 1962

The Considerate Man

I will begin by placing my subject in a particular situation at a particular time, so that, through his words and deeds, we may get a clearer picture of him. After all, the only way to truly judge people is to observe them in relation to particular occasions and to make mental notes of their behaviour patterns during these specified times. Therefore I will choose for my hour the dinner hour and for my situation a crowded table with one able-bodied woman tending to the needs of all. To begin with, it is not an uncommon situation. Hence the main reason for my selection.

Caps are placed across knees or on the backs of chairs and the merry clatter of cutlery rises above the small talk. She starts out by decorating the table-centre with a large dish of spuds. She follows this with a large dish of vegetables and finally she places before each man a large plate of meat. All accept graciously with subdued words of thanks with the honourable exception of the considerate man.

When his plate is filled with meat, spuds and vegetables, he looks around him before he eats and addresses the woman of the house as follows: 'Are you going to sit down at all yourself?'

In his heart, he doesn't care whether she does or not and in a sense he is the conscience of his fellows. They resent him, however, because they forgot to offer the suggestion themselves. All know that it would not be possible for her to take a seat until the wants of the men are fulfilled and anyway there is no room for her at the table but there is always a considerate chap who asks the inevitable question: 'What about your dinner?' Having said this he does not wait for her to reply but attacks the contents of his plate with justification and satisfaction. He has eased his conscience and pulled a fast one on his co-grubbers. He also has a head-start on the spuds as the rest are temporarily preoccupied with genuine consideration for the woman.

He is at his best, however, when going on a car journey. 'Sit back here,' he says, 'you'll be more comfortable', knowing full well that there is a draught in that particular part of the car.

At wakes he excels. The kitchen is crowded with mourners and seats are taken up. A relative of the deceased arrives late and the minute he sees her he shouts: ' Someone get up, in the honour of God, and let the poor woman sit down!' he never gets up himself. Somebody else always does but it is he who gets the credit.

His consideration knows no bound when he is without a seat himself. He will advise one of the household to have a good night's sleep pointing out that no one can stay up forever. It usually works and when the victim departs our friend immediately occupies his chair.

I met one of these considerate individuals for the first time in the bog during the Second World War. I was in sole charge of the tea-making but it was our friend who distributed the bread and cold bacon.

'Here!' he said, handing me a piece of the fat; 'you're as thin as a match. This is the stuff to fatten you!' I noticed that he kept the lean pieces for himself although he was as thin as I was. For instance if there were three slices of bread and a crust left between four of us, he would always hand me the crust, saying: 'Here! You like the crust!'

He was always making sacrifices. Cigarettes were scarce and so were matches. When a breeze blew, it was difficult to light a butt. Once he snapped the cigarettes and matches from my hand. 'Show me those,' he said, 'and I'll light it for you.' During the lighting ceremony, he always consumed half the cigarette.

The world is full of considerate men who are always doing good unto others.

Once, at a race meeting, when I was young, I stood on a box vainly attempting to see the finish of a steeplechase in which I had invested a shilling. Suddenly I was seized from behind by a long, rangy countryman.

'You'll get kilt up on top of that!' he said and with great alacrity he jumped on the box himself and had the additional effrontery to lean heavily on my shoulder to watch the closing stages of the race.

Even in church, one is not safe from the considerate man. At a retreat, when I was about thirteen, a man with a soft round face assisted me from my position at the end of a crowded pew. 'Shove up farther,' he said; 'you'll hear nothin' there!' The next thing I knew he had my seat and was staring away into space with the most angelic of countenances. It happens, too, in queues for the confessional. A considerate man once stepped in front of me and said: 'I'll go in front of you and soften him out for you!'

Even with experienced adults, they'll try anything if they think they can get away with it. Many years ago, I was commissioned by a country woman to carry a small roll of tarpaulin to her pony and trap. A considerate man, on the make for the price of a pint, accompanies me without being invited. When we were nearing the trap, he said: 'show me that tarpaulin. 'Tis too heavy for you.' He took it from my shoulder, deposited it in the trap, collected a shilling and was gone before I knew what had taken place.

Sept 1966

Onions

Recently, while passing a shop window, I saw hanging inside a string of golden onions.

I passed a month later and there hung the same string, undamaged and unchanged by the passage of time. Surely a remarkable accomplishment for that which is neither fruit nor vegetable. Who but this pungent edible bulb could improve with age and who is less conscious of its serenity, durability, and dignity? There were bananas, worthy fellows, exhibited on the same window and there were peaches and pears but they thing that caught the eye was the string of onions.

Onion, who has flanked and flavoured the proud steak and strengthened its munificent aromas. Onion who has buttressed the frivolous chop enlarging its exuberant vitality. Onion who has ennobled the quivering liver sliver oft mistreated by repeated overturnings. Onion who has feted fecund tripe and sanctified the most sentient of gravies. Onion, with the saliva on my chin, I salute you! I, my friends and my foes, are indebted to you. To you we owe the monumental and relieving belch and the smooth running of the myriad meticulous machinations which occupy our unexplored interiors.

We will not readily forget your right hand in the warring with the porter-conscious matrons for often you have saved us, repeatedly concealing the cataclysmic odour of booze and tempering the malt-laden breath with life-saving camouflage of indigenous versatility. Onion, lowly onion, inured to trial by vegetation. Onion, you have carried mashed potatoes on your back and in bread-stuffing you were the body and soul of the mixture, overpowering stale bread and crusts with indignant whiffs and pauperising parsley with detached superiority. So, let it be with stale bread.

Outnumbered in every possible concoction, you have more than held your own, accounted for yourself without bombast or advertisement, and put mightier names to shame when performance was the only criterion.

Wars will be fought but in the end nothing will be resolved and the old injustices ripen as before, but, onion, you were there before them and you will be there after them. Let them make little of you, but you were never governed. No culinary smell dared to usurp you. Onion, prince, oft disparaged by worthless contumely of leek and lettuce and even awed by burly hearted cabbage – none of them possess your soul. Onion, oft unloved and unestablished still, despite the contribution you have made to countless broths. Onion, oft maligned by lesser entities, in spite of assistance rendered to soups of all sorts, in spite of flavour loaned to unnumbered and uncited stews. In sandwiches, weak apologies for mealtime, you were ever-present. In every trail you stood apart. You were the body and soul of all your allies. You were more! You were yourself, which millions strive to be and, failing, snub you. Onion, cannon of the dispossessed, battlement of the downtrodden, succour of the starving. Fools know you and take you for their own. Kings and emperors adopt you. Flung you were in rage from turrets at the oppressor's head and stripped you were in awful nudity to combat the overpowering smell of paint. Thrust you were into the cavernous bosoms of hanging turkeys and, chopped into scintillating dices, encouraging the poor beef and kidney stew. You have the mighty egg confounded with flavour potent and the back rasher confounded with toothsome deliciousness.

Onion, you are well worth watching and will bear watching always. On sheds of corrugated iron and strung from henhouse doors you have faced the summer heat but yet expiry never neared you. The bestial frosts of harvest were as putty in your hands. The winter winds and rains taunted you in vain. Their worst could not subdue you. The sun you loved above all others, and he, to show his feelings, clothed you in raiment of gold. You shone and bristled in the corded bags of fruiterers. When all fruit fails, there is the onion, and fruit you are in truth and tuber, too. No bough of tender garden free your likeness ever bore. No pear or peach or plum could match your glowing symmetry. The Irish stew without you is an empty lifeless mess.

Onion, indispensable onion, no housewife dare forget you, no haughty chef has courage to ignore you. Consigned to earthen pit like common fare you did emerge untarnished, glimmering all over like freshly minted gold. Penny, the lowliest of coins, will purchase you. Rare sovereigns will accomplish nothing better, your breath is as the breath of time. No swirling planet is your peer and yet no poet has taken up his pen to do you justice. Onion, you are the poem and the poet in one, the lyric and the lyricist, the singer and the song. Your monument is your seed.

I hail you and salute you, indefatigable onion!

Dec 62

On Pandy

Let porter fresh from laughing barrels
Abolish life's unending quarrels
And if there's plates and saucers handy
Fill up the lot with steaming pandy.

ANONYMOUS

The unknown ballad-maker who put these lines together will not be remembered for his contribution to the annals of great poetry, but he will be remembered with some pride and affection by men who liked pandy. He will be quoted by moist-eyed men who are not ashamed of their backgrounds. I have nothing personal against the use of bread-stuffing in roast fowls. Each to his own taste. Let there be no bitterness or misunderstanding. I am only doing what must be done.

I want merely, from a feeling of national conscience, to denude bread-stuffing of much of its grandeur and glamour and give it the status it deserves. Surely nothing could be fairer than that and after all what is bread-stuffing but the transformation of stale bread into an unattractive mess, acceptable to those who do not know any better. It is fraudulent. I am not being deliberately provocative or endeavouring to stir up controversy but I have strong feelings about this particular subject. It was the harbinger of rock 'n' roll, the atom bomb and the bikini. To the truly fastidious, it is totally unacceptable. To the now almost extinct species of open-hearted or convivial Irish gourmand, it will never usurp potato-stuffing. I should, of course, have said 'pandy' but in these days of diced potatoes, there is a certain wariness in expressing natural sentiments publicly.

'Pandy', the only bi-syllabic word likely to replace the infantile 'da-da'; pandy – like the deliciously sentimental songs of Foster – is threatened by the ephemeral fads of today. Let those who want mashed potatoes have mashed potatoes but I will not condone a dry white mass devoid of onions, milk and butter. What good is bread-stuffing to hands that are calloused by plough-handles, or to men who work in offices all day?

Things have come to a terrible pass. It is no longer wise in certain societies to express longing for a grilled red herring. The mention of black puddings and home-made drisheens is taboo. Even periwinkles are frowned upon. What I would like to ask is – who is to blame? It is a matter that I would like to take up with those responsible. If the word 'pandy' is mentioned, it is done in whispers by the kind-faced middle-aged men who remember with moist eyes a mother's cry from yesterday: 'Your pandy is on the table, dear; come in before 'tis cold!'

I am not campaigning for a return to the old ways. Much of what is new is good. All I ask for is a minor concession. I appeal to the young housewife. There is no greater joy than chasing a small boy who has absconded with a fistful of exposed pandy from the goose she is basting.

How many are left who remember the great delights of yesterday? I would like to know the man who was not moved at the sight of steaming buds of pandy bursting through the seams in the waistcoat pockets of a juicy goose. I will throw caution to the winds and go further. I would like to meet him personally and hear him out to the end of his prejudice. I am not a fighting man, but I will not be pushed.

One thing leads to another. Bread-stuffing leads to a wine list. A wine list calls for knowledge, which is the least; also considerable cash, which is the most. Pandy does not need to be buttressed. Like the lighthouse, it stands alone.

I am not wholly blaming this new generation for the threat to pandy. The portents were evident a long time ago. The Egyptians, the Greeks, the Romans and the Irish held that fair warning was always given before the advent of decline. Warning in this case was given, unless I am greatly mistaken, when began the inconsiderate placing of forks to the left of a person and knives to the right. The left-handed man was not considered here. This was the first threat to the individual; the first instance of a similar treatment for the masses. Here the human spirit must rebel. We have been pushed far enough. A stand must be made somewhere. The black pudding has been reduced to garbage level. The red herring has been consigned to the night-watchman. Pandy will shortly be associated with a certain trade or profession. It may be yours. If we are to make a stand, what nobler one than in defence of pandy.

Feb 1961

In Search of People

How to attract the attention of one person without attracting the attention of others is a task so delicate and so fraught with bewildering repercussions that it should be entrusted only to shrewd and experiences couriers. The complications which arise from the most elementary missions in this respect would fill a good-sized book.

My first introduction to a situation of this kind was at the local cinema. A neighbour of ours, a young woman of excitable disposition, found herself, after a walk one evening, to be without her latch-key. My mother who was a great believer in the good neighbour policy, commissioned me to climb into the backyard of the woman's house and, from there, to make every effort to gain admission to this house itself.

I did my part of the job but the rear of the house was so skilfully defended against intrusion that my mission was fruitless. I reported back and confessed defeat.

'The last hope now,' said the woman, 'is that himself might be at the pictures.'

Again, I was commissioned.

I left post haste and arrived within minutes at the local cinema, which was locked up, since the film was well under way within. After a bout of knocking had failed, I kicked the door several times as hard as I could, and finally a man appeared. He was very annoyed. I told him the identity of the man I wanted without saying what I wanted him for.

'He's in the house all right,' said the doorman, 'but you'll have to wait till I get a light.'

So saying, he disappeared and returned with the biggest flashlamp I had ever seen.

'Come on,' he said, 'and we'll find him.'

Inside the darkened hall, he switched on the lamp and then he moved from row to row, followed by myself. He shone the light into every face, without apology, and there was great commotion. Women gasped and men held up their hands before their faces to shield themselves. At last, he located his man.

'You're wanted home at once!' he said. 'Your wife needs you!'

There was a tone of impeachment in his voice and, as I had by now grown accustomed to the darkened hall, I could detect looks of contempt and derision on the faces of the other patrons. But who could blame them? Here was a man enjoying himself at the pictures while his wife waited at home in desperate need of him. Some instinct told me that the time had come for me to disappear. Later I learned that there were some words when he got home and he and his spouse were not on speaking terms for the following three days.

Man is unquestionably gifted with the powers of imagination and reason but when he sees one of his fellows being called away out of a crowd, his reason deserts him and he uses his imagination for all he's worth.

Once, at a dance, the band-leader came to the microphone and announced that Johnny So-and-So was wanted home immediately. The truth of the matter was that he had ducked out of home without doing his lessons and his parents dispatched his younger sister to find him. She was an excitable girl and, instead of standing near the door and discreetly beckoning to him while he passed during a dance, she instead notified the management who, in turn, notified the leader of the band. Band-leaders have a strong sense of the dramatic and they must be forgiven if they make the most of such opportunities.

At the time I was dancing with a red-haired girl, a nifty quickstepper, who is since married and the mother of five children. When she heard the announcement she turned to another girl and said: 'His grandmother must be dead!'

I personally knew the grandmother, who lived in the house with the young man's parents. She had been sick the previous week. Quickly the word spread around the hall and, as the young man left, couples of his acquaintance pressed their sympathy on him. At the doorway, he met his sister who was sixteen and a year younger than he. She told him he was wanted home to do his lessons. He assured her that they were done. A short, whispered exchange followed and, as a result, brother and sister joined in the dance and, I must say, they made a very nice couple indeed.

The other dancers were horrified, since they had no way of knowing that the grandmother was alive and kicking and destined to outlive many of those present on the occasion. Eventually the young man and his sister were approached by a tall, well-built chap of thirty or so. He began by giving the student a hefty puck in the back and finished by escorting the student and his sister, each by an arm, from the hall.

These two examples should serve as a warning to would-be messengers. Discretion is imperative, so that if some day you should be sent in search of, say, me, do it cutely. A nod will do and you will find me only too eager to listen to what you have to say.

References

There is nothing as tricky as writing a reference, or being asked to write a reference, and last Thursday when a man came to see me on what he termed a matter of grave importance, I knew I was once again faced with the same dilemma.

'I want you,' he said, 'to ketch a hoult of your pen and make out a reference for my daughter.'

'I don't know you,' I said, 'and I don't know your daughter.'

'I know,' he said, 'but I hear great accounts of you as a writer.'

The writing of references was once the dubious prerogative of priests and schoolmasters and it was necessary to be the possessor of a good one from both if one wanted to get a job as a domestic, a clerk, or a civil servant. References were never needed for agricultural or county council workers. This, I daresay, was because they were so paid so little and the best reference they could possibly own was a willingness to work from dawn till dark on as little food and pay as possible. In fact, if a farmer's boy could be found who ate nothing at all, his stomach would be his reference.

But I digress! Where was I, anyway?

Yes! I have in my time come across some unusual references and one in particular comes to mind which was a priceless piece of forgery and a work of art in its own way. It was given to me by a young man who could neither read nor write and who wanted it to begin a career as a barman. It was written on the back of a ballad which, as far as I can remember, was 'The Valley of Knockanure' and it contained the following: 'Behold I am with you all the days even unto the consummation of the world', and it was signed 'Matthew'.

'But,' I told him, 'this is of no use to you as a reference!'

'That's a shame,' he said, 'after I spending the most of an hour taking it down.'

'Where did you get it?' I asked.

'I got it,' he said, 'from a tombstone above at the bottom of the churchyard, for,' he went on, 'there's always some good written on top about the man that's underneath.'

All he wanted me to do was to add another bit on to it, as he considered it too short. 'You can leave the man's name that wrote it at the bottom,' he said.

'Fair enough!' I said and I played Paul to his Matthew. 'Take a little wine for thy stomach's sake,' I wrote, 'and for thy frequent infirmities.'

'There's no Christian,' he said finally, 'would turn down a man with a reference like this!'

The first reference I ever got was from one of my old National School teachers. It was a good one and I still have it. The second was more difficult. I was obliged to get one from the canon of the time, now deceased, God rest him! I went to the presbytery door after mass and asked the house-keeper if I might see him.

'You came at a bad time,' she said, 'but I'll call him out anyway.'

He came out, gave one scathing look at me, and then suddenly inquired: 'How long since your last confession?'

I told him and then he asked: 'Is the girl from the parish?'

I had great difficulty in persuading him that I didn't want

to get married. I was thirteen years of age at the time. He took me into his study and wrote out the reference. He handed it to me and said: 'don't leave it go too long. A fellow like you would want to be settling down and have someone to look after you.'

Times have changed, however, and letters of reference no longer have a significant influence. The tendency these days is to suggest the name of a referee who may be contacted to give an account and description of the candidate or applicant. Gone forever are the happy days when the letter began: 'I have known this boy all his life ...' and went on to eulogise the subject ending on a note of such supreme confidence in the person in question that the candidate sounded more like a candidate for canonisation than for a clerkship.

These old-time references were just too good to be true with their abundance of colourful adjectives. There were fine descriptive passages too, like, 'of sober and temperate habits, of ingenious and industrious outlook, of outstanding honesty and integrity, possesses a brilliant future and will be of inestimable assistance to anybody who is fortunate enough to secure his services.'

Ah, those were the fine sentences and it is a pity that they should be lost to us forever. Only the other day I heard of a young man who had the gumption and originality to say goodbye forever to references and submit a testimonial.

A Christmas Encounter

Last week I was forced, against my better judgement, to indulge in some pre-Christmas shopping.

There was a large crowd in the town in question and freedom of movement was restricted. At last I saw what I wanted – a nice quiet shop, where the girls behind the counter spoke in subdued voices.

'I would like,' I said, 'to see some jumpers, size 40.'

Without a word, the girl turned to her shelves, paused, rearranged her hair and surveyed her stocks.

'What you want,' she said after a while, 'is a nice twin-set.'

'No,' I reminded her, 'I want a jumper.'

She threw some boxes on the counter, in front of me, and deftly removed the covers.

'Would you mind,' she said, 'not smoking. The ash falls on the garments.'

'These are not garments,' I told her. 'These are polo-necked jumpers and they are not what I want. What I want is a v-necked jumper.'

'What size do you want?' she asked.

'All right; all right,' I told her. 'I'll take a twin-set.'

More boxes appeared but she wouldn't let me take the article I wanted.

'Mustard is all the go these days,' she said.

'I don't know all about that, Miss. I was in a hotel a while ago and they had no mustard.'

'It's the colour I'm talking about,' she explained.

Finally, after an age, she gave me the twin-set which suited her and I paid up.

In the street, with my parcel under my arm, I dodged hurrying passers-by. I went into another shop and called for a bottle of perfume. The assistant was obliging enough and I was just about to make a purchase when the boss appeared on the scene and suggested a new perfume which had just come on the market.

'You might have seen it advertised,' he said.

I confessed I hadn't. He shooed the assistant away. When, in the end, I opted for the original bottle of perfume he beamed all over as if it had been his idea, while the assistant stood morosely in the background pretending to rearrange lipstick samples. I felt guilty about the whole affair. Again, I paid and left without saying goodbye.

Out on the crowded street once more, which by now was jammed with people of all shapes and sizes, a man confronted me.

'I know you!' he said.

He wore a long brown coat and cap and under his oxter he carried a brown paper parcel with blood seeping through one of its corners.

'A bit o' mate for tomorrow's dinner,' he explained. 'As we met,' he went on, 'we'll have to have a drink.'

Away we went into a crowded public house.

'You'll have something short?' he said.

'I don't mind if I do,' I agreed.

He called for two half-whiskeys and we sat down, the better to enjoy them. We had two more and we discovered that we had mutual acquaintances. There was an aunt of his married back my way and a first cousin of my own bought a farm near his. I rose and called for two more half ones. We smoked and chatted about a variety of subjects.

'Do you ever go to the races?' he enquired.

I told him that I did, occasionally, and he gave me a tip for a horse. Time passed and we decided that it was time to depart. We walked up the street together, avoiding the bustling passers-by.

'You know,' he said, 'somehow you look a different man since we had the few drinks.'

'I was going to say the same thing to you,' I said, 'because somehow you look different too.'

'It's amazing, isn't it,' he said, 'the difference two drinks can make in a man.'

'There's more to it than that,' I pointed out philosophically. 'We didn't know each other too well before and now we're on friendly terms. People look different when you get to know them better.'

'I have it figured out,' he said, and he stopped and pointed a finger to the place where brains are supposed to be. 'The difference is that we both has parcels when we first met and we haven't any parcels now.'

We retraced our steps hurriedly and there were the parcels sitting side by side on the table where we had deposited them. We both agreed that it was remarkable to find so much honesty in the world.

'I wouldn't mind your parcel not being stolen,' my friend explained, 'because nobody could tell what's in it, but mine is different because obviously it's a parcel of mate and a parcel of mate in a public house is a terrible temptation.'

He went on to tell me that it is fair game to pick up a parcel of meat in a public house.

'I often lost two parcels in the one day,' he confided, 'but a parcel often came my way too.'

'Poetic justice!' I explained.

'Justice or no justice,' he said, 'we'll have another drink. What's yours?'

We both had bottles of stout and again we sat down.

'For the life of me,' he whispered, 'I couldn't go into a shop to buy a present. The missus does all that. I'll buy mate all right but don't send me looking for fol de dols because I'll have to refuse you.'

We had two more bottles of stout.

'Do you drive?' he asked.

'No,' I replied. 'Do you?'

'I wouldn't know what to do if you put me in a car.'

We finished our drinks and rose to go. This time we did not forget our parcels.

'A happy Christmas to you,' I said and shook his hand.

'The same to you,' he said.

'Is there anything wrong?' I asked, for I had noticed that he was looking at me in a peculiar fashion.

'Nothing,' he said, 'except that you have my parcel and I have yours!'

Dec 1966

The Phone and the Flu

Scrawled in frost across the window-panes was a badly-written letter from winter. I decided not to answer it so I pulled the clothes tightly under my chin and rapped four times on the wall. A prearranged code message this, to show that I was awake and ready for my morning capsule. One every four hours the doctor had said. The call is answered, the capsule consumed and at the mercy of an unimpaired digestive tract when the phone rings.

There is nobody in the house now. The missus has gone for the meat and this is the girl's morning off. I decide to ignore it but it persists like a hungry baby so I dash out of bed.

'Who's speaking?'

'Is Anne there?' a man's voice says.

'No,' I say, 'she won't be in till evening.'

'Is she going to Lixnaw tonight?' the voice asks.

'Look!' I tell him, 'I have the flu and am under doctor's orders.'

Then follows a silence.

'Who's speaking?' I ask again.

'Ah, don't mind that,' says the voice, 'but tell her the fellow she met at the Angler's Dance in Listowel rang up and he's going to Lixnaw tonight.'

'All right!' I promised. 'I'll tell her when she comes in but maybe she won't remember you.'

At this he laughed knowingly, reminding me of George Saunders.

'There's no doubt,' I said, 'but you fancy yourself,' and I prepared to hang up but he beat me to the punch.

'Some of us has it,' he said, 'and more hasn't!'

In bed, it took a while before I warmed up and just as I began to feel relatively comfortable, the phone rang again. I won't be caught this time, I told myself, and I pulled the clothes over my head. It is no easy matter to drown out the sound of a demanding telephone. I got out of bed but this time I put on my slippers, and overcoat and a scarf. If I'd had a hat I'd have out that on too.

I lifted the receiver and asked for the identity of the speaker. It was a woman's voice and immediately she gave her name. Equally fast was her question.

'What do you think of corporal punishment?' she said.

'I'm all for it,' I told her, 'provided it's administered to people who get other people out of bed needlessly.'

We parted on unfriendly terms and I wisely took the phone off the hook. That'll fix 'em, I told myself.

After that, I dozed for a while and woke when there was a knock at the door. The doctor entered and took my pulse and temperature. He scrutinised the thermometer and shook his head.

'Down to a hundred!' he said triumphantly.

'Can I get up?' I asked.

'Out of the question!' he said.

'But I'm in bed now,' I said, 'for four days and there's no improvement. My nose is blocked and I can't taste my food.

He consoled me and wrote out another prescription, this time for different capsules. Time passed and I ate some of my dinner. Apart from the loss of taste, I heartily dislike dinner in bed. It gives me heartburn and I dislike heartburn. Win, lose or draw, I told myself, I'm getting up tomorrow and, which is more, I'm staying up. I began to miss the company of my friends and since I am addicted to a pint or two at night I longed for the sociable hum of conversation and I was beginning to miss the prevailing gossip. I dislike porter in bed. Maybe it has something to do with violent contrasts. The black of the porter and the white of the pillowcase are extreme opposites and always create conflict within me. The porter isn't the same either. It tastes like watery soup and, anyway, I am a man who cannot drink a pint while on the flat of my back. Sitting down is all right but standing up in my favourite position.

I called out to find out what time it was and the missus entered to say it was half past ten. She asked me how I was feeling and I told her I wasn't too bad but that I couldn't taste anything and that my nose was blocked, that I had a pain in the head and in the chest and that there was water coming out of my eyes.

'You're just in the middle of it now,' she said. 'Another three or four days and you'll be grand.'

She left and I thought about this and became somewhat despondent. I have nothing against beds providing I am tired but when I feel that life is going on without me, I chafe at the bit and am inclined to be irritable.

The minutes went wearily by and though I noticed the contours of bulky uneven clouds as they piled endlessly across the sky intimidating the frost and ending its icy reign with aggressive raindrops. The phone rang again and I knew it must be an intimate friend. So it was.

'I heard you had the flu?' he said.

'A touch of it,' I replied.

'That's a pity!' he said.

'Why is it a pity?' I asked.

'Ah, well,' he said, 'I was thinking of going to Newcastle West coursing and I thought you might like to come.'

I thought for a moment and while I was thinking he said: 'A change of air is a great cure for influenza.'

I took him at his word and soon we were on our way. My 'flu disappeared and I haven't been afflicted with it since.

The moral is that if you're in bed and able to get up, do so until you have to go back to bed again.

Men Who Go Off It

This is the season of waverers and wishful thinkers, for now the vows of the New Year have become impossible burdens and none but men of inflexible determination are holding fast.

For many, the rash promises of January first have proved an exemplary lesson. It has taught them that only a fool shoulders more than he can carry and that a man with a natural tooth for porter should never say: 'I will go off the pint for good', but rather: 'I will go off the pint for as long as I can'.

We are not all men of iron, but we have in common with each other an unbridled belief in our limited capabilities. After the first few weeks of being 'on the dry' many fall by the wayside, but these men must not be derided for at least they have tried, and those more steely fellows who point the finger of scorn at the less fortitudinous should remember that the other four fingers are pointing at themselves.

I am not condoning the habits of the consistent drinker. Far from it. I am merely trying to make a case for the hard-working man who has surrendered his privileges without qualification. When a man goes off it there are other temptations. He is forced into picture houses away from the company of his friends. He is compelled to invest in sleeping draughts and pills, for insomnia is the greatest curse attached to the variety of deprivation. He expects tea and biscuits before retiring and I am told of some who held out for Swiss rolls and sponge-cake.

The old likeable character who came in from the pub at night to deliver the news of the day, is now replaced by a demanding crank. The easily-pleased, healthy fellow who did not care whether he got crusts or currant loaf is gone and he is sadly missed, although nobody will admit it, and while it may seem that he is relatively happy, he is in fact far from well. In his heart he is crying for the sight of a pint and longing for the faces of his old associates. Every time he passes a pub he turns his head away and whenever he hears the tinkle of glasses his ears twitch like a greyhound's at the sight of a hare. He lags at conversation and he, who was once the most talkative of all, is now reserved and silent, for there is nothing to loosen his tongue and nothing to expand his heart.

I am reminded of a simple man whose constitution went wrong and whose sleep was destroyed when he went off the pint. He quickly went on it again, to the disgust of his household. Being a man who liked to see his home happy, he consulted a wiser man and placed his difficulties before him. 'My friend,' said the wise man, 'you are suffering from a disease known as "porter-tooth" and until such time as this tooth is pulled you will not be able to exist without porter.'

Our simple friend went to a dentist and asked that the offender be extracted from his gums.

'Now,' said the dentist, 'will you tell me which tooth is the "porter-tooth"?'

'I don't know,' my friend replied.

'In that case,' said the dentist, 'I will begin at the bottom left and keep pulling until the tooth in question is removed.'

So, the dentist pulled one tooth but the desire for porter still remained. He pulled another and another and finally when he had pulled them all, he asked his patient if he was cured.

'It don't look like it,' my friend answered, 'because I never had more mind for a pint than I have this minute.'

'I'm afraid,' the dentist said, 'that you were wrongly advised, for I'm inclined to believe that the tooth in question is a psychological tooth, and the cure is surely worse than the disease. I suffer from the same disease myself and the only consolation I can offer is to invite you to join me over a pint in the pub across the street.'

The porter-tooth is a tooth of the mind. In some men it is dormant, in others volcanic, and in most men it is nearly always exposed. Nobody can advise those who suffer from this malady and a man must look into himself for the cure. The answer may be in a vaccine and those who aspire to the Nobel Prize would be well advised to look into the matter without delay, since the incidence of the disease is of shocking proportions and a source of constant worry to those who do not suffer from it.

To stress the extraordinary heroism of men who go 'off it' for however brief a period I would like to take a particular subject and present a brief case history of his plight. He is a normal enough man, married with a family perhaps. He is a solid worker. He is a reader, but only of newspapers, and he is a sportsman because he is capable of shouting insults at the referee during football matches. He is a good enough provider and his family has never known want. His house is safe and solid and his insurance is paid up. He gets on well with his neighbours and is liked by his fellows. He is a good father and a good husband and he has a mind of his own. He is fond of a few pints, particularly on a Saturday night. He is a good man in a chorus and particularly effective in 'The Hills of Donegal'. This, I think, is a fair picture of the man in normal circumstances.

Then he decides to go 'off it' for a number of reasons. The change is hardly noticeable at first, but after a while he is seen to be absent-minded and at times he is caught red-handed looking out of the kitchen window with a faraway look in his eyes. Then he begins to complain of minor happenings, such a neighbour's child crying in the night, or the way his meat is fried. He is irritable if somebody else reads the paper before he does and angry if the collars of his shirt are not perfectly ironed. Life seems to hold no future for him.

He is, as you will gather, a changed man, but the answer does not lie within himself, as so many believe. The answer lies with the woman he married, who knows him better than anybody else, and who loves him into the bargain, and it may happen that she will end his suffering one Saturday evening when she says: 'In the honour o' God, wouldn't you go out and drink a few pints and not be moping there like an old woman!'

Jan 1963

Courting

I couldn't court no more nor a crow!

OVERHEARD

Of all the ingenious forms of sport devised by man since his creation, courting remains the most intriguing and the most popular.

In practice, it has changed little, and in theory it hasn't changed at all. Football teams have been reduced from twenty-one to fifteen, but in courting the number of sides remains the same, each team consisting of a solitary competitor. The only difference is that there is no need for a referee since the participants are always most agreeably disposed towards each other.

Recently I asked an old man from Athea if there were any substantial changes in the tactics employed since his day.

'There's no change,' he said, 'but in my time we usedn't meet so often, and you mightn't see a girl for the length of a week.'

'Do you think it's a bad thing,' I asked, 'if boys and girls meet too often?'

'Ah, man,' said he, 'sure you couldn't meet girls often enough and the girls are the same way inclined towards the boys, because when I was a young man if I failed to turn up in Athea for a dance, you'd hear the girls ullagoning as far away as Templeglantine.'

Courting is the most delicate of subjects and, not being

an authority, I am somewhat reluctant about declaiming its subtleties to any great extent. I possess a limited knowledge, of course, and might, like many others, be described as proficient had it not been for the impatience of hackney-drivers in such a hurry home after dances that one would think they had never courted themselves.

Courting is the chief textbook for marriage but its beginnings are a far cry from the wedding breakfast and the honeymoon. I remember in my youth it was the practice to walk as often as possible past the house where the creature of the moment lived. It was also the practice to blush furiously and cross to the other side of the street if she happened to appear. This might be described as a phase. Another phase is the period of complete dependence upon intermediaries who as often as not, according to the lie of the land, are likely to present their own cases before those of their clients.

Then there is the communal in public phase when crowds of boys frolic with crowds of girls. There is the calf-love or the mooning phase when a chap with the appetite of a horse eats only four potatoes instead of the usual five. This is the last of the childhood phases and the next step is quite a jump from wall scribbling and tree-carving and note-writing because it is in the next few years that the inevitable decision must be made unless one is to remain a permanent pursuer or bachelor, which is the kind term acceded these gentlemen by inaccurate and hastily-compiled dictionaries.

A man should make the most of these years without resorting to flippancy, because if he wants to boast in middle age about the great number of women who adored him he must make the most of his available time before the right woman comes along to terminate his insularity. This is the time for immaculate collars, fancy socks, bright waistcoats, hair oil and close shaves, the time for testing the suitability of all available candidates for the permanent position which is about to be offered. It is the crucial stage, for if he waits he will wilt and, being wilted, will have nothing to choose from but other wilted flowers like himself.

Courting should be the stepping-stone to the permanent liaison, not a dalliance for nit-wits and protractors. It should be an unsparing effort to discover whose kisses are the most desirable, whose voice the most melodious and whose manner the most endearing.

There eventually comes a time when parties are fully committed. This happens after an established process has been completed and what began with the mere offer of a lift to work ends in the present of a dressing gown for her birthday and a twin-set for Christmas, for it is practical presents like these that denote the ultimate possibility of a wedding ring. Presents of a minor nature, such as earrings, brooches, writing sets and perfumes, are always acceptable, but they lack the intimidating and aggressive possessiveness conveyed by the well-chosen garment, not that I am supporting the flimsy claim of headscarfs and 12/11 nylons, but weighty gifts like three-quarter-length suede coats and fur wraps have been known to make a disinterested girl interested.

Much has been written and said about kissing, with no resultant degree of conclusiveness. Kissing is the essence of courtship, and the best judge of a kiss is the recipient. Hand-holding, while certainly touching, has on occasion been held up to ridicule and its practice is best confined to dark places like cinemas and quiet places like river banks, or, if you are poetically inclined, to dells where grows the bluebell. Daisy-chain making is strictly for novices, but the odd picnic is not to be laughed off and friends of mine have even paddled in streams with their chosen ones. Cheek-to-cheek dancing is a sure sign that wedding bells are being cast in the moulding departments of twin minds and those who go home early from dances are toying with the idea of perpetual partnership.

Spring is with us again and with it has come a new crop of boys and girls who will cross paths in the summertime, so if the gangling youth of yesterday suddenly appears with his hair creased and his ears washed, you will know that he has girls on his mind.

Feb 1963

Crying

But where are all the loves of long ago.
Oh, little ship of twilight, blown up the tide,
Where are the faces laughing in the glow
Of morning years, the lost ones scattered wide!
Give me your hand, my brother, let us go
Crying down the dark for those who died.

FRANCIS LEDWIDGE

The man who cannot cry has not been brought up properly, or else the well of tears is too deep for words.

I had a good cry recently.

I went to Dublin on business and afterwards I met a brother of mine who works there. Having met, we repaired to a public house and had a few drinks. We left and visited a bookshop. We had our tea at a well-known hostelry and afterwards went to see a play. Between the acts, we hastily visited a hotel in the immediate vicinity of the playhouse, where we indulged in the usual. The play finished and we repaired to my hotel. We talked about old things and resurrected the heroic incidents of childhood. There was no boyhood like ours and we shook our heads at the loveless spirit of present-day families. We spoke about hero-worship and solved each other's problems. When the time came to go we both cried. My analytical mind told me that the drink we had consumed was responsible, but my heart dictated the truth.

'Stop that crying!' I told him.

'A bit of a cry is good,' he said, putting his handkerchief back into his pocket and his hand around my shoulder.

Oh, the laughable things we cry at!

The cry is a first cousin to the laugh, and, to tell you the truth, I hadn't a good cry with ages, but wouldn't it be an awful world if there was nothing to cry about, or if some autocratic state instituted a by-law which might forbid crying.

Nothing is so laughable as the things we cry at. I have seen detached people crying at funerals and wakes just because they came along for a bit of a cry, whereas the people who were afflicted by terrible loss weren't able to cry at all. The older we get the less we cry and the older we get the less we laugh, because the world and experience, inimitable teachers that they are, are utterly divorced from the heart.

My first memory of crying is watching my mother's face. Who knows from what fountain her tears sprung. It was enough that she was crying, and her example put me crying, too.

An infant cries because of hunger, loneliness or fear. A kiss or a hug or a kind word can easily dismiss the torment of a child. It does not matter who owns him. With the larger boy, what matters is that he may be crying in his mind while his face forces a smile.

A good pat on the back is a great cure for crying, but there are times when it can be dangerous to stop a person from crying. I once tried it with my wife when she was reminiscing about her father, who is dead. I acted the clown and, when that failed, I kissed her. It was no good and I shouldn't have tried. She needed to cry.

Coming down Patrick Street one morning a few years

ago, I saw a woman crying as she looked at a shop window. 'Maybe she has no money,' I argued in my mind, 'or maybe something she has seem reminds her of someone who is dead and she is turning her face here to the window to keep it from a curious crowd. Maybe she's after getting a fiver from her husband who has worked overtime and she's grateful to him that it's only now she can pay God for what He has done for the lot of them.' What matters most is that she needed to cry and she, God help her, could not choose the time or the place.

In my own world of writing, I am often tempted to cry, and by cry, I don't mean tears, because a man will cry without tears when he finds things going against him. I often wished I could cry and I often wished I could laugh. The only difference between the two is the least recognised of shading.

To those who have often felt like crying I would say – cry! By all means, cry! The tears are your own and the sorrow is nearly always for somebody else.

A couple I know have two small boots on their mantelpiece. The wearer is dead. Every time they look at these infinitesimal boots they laugh, but the important thing is that sometimes they cry as well.

When you've read this, go and have a good cry if you've something to cry about, and don't shut yourself away from your own crowd; or otherwise a small boy might never learn how to cry.

We all have tears inside of us and this shouldn't be so, because faces are developed out of smiles and the relief that comes from crying.

March 1963

Blushing

Man is the only animal that blushes,
And the only animal with reason to blush.

MARK TWAIN

When a person loses the capacity for blushing life is no longer the teacher.

The blush is the reaction of the word or deed that pricks the conscience, and the blush is the spontaneous reply of innocence when glibness catches it unawares.

A blush is a glow caused by shame or modesty. So the dictionaries would have us believe. But I have seen glows on faces and the cause was neither modesty nor shame. I have seen purple noses attached to vermilion dials and both owed their colouring to nothing more than repeated doses of guaranteed pot-still whiskey. I have seen scarlet faces etched by the artistry of roast beef and boiled bacon, whose owners have chosen to ignore the treachery of blood pressure and prefer a short but tempestuous existence to a long and bloodless one.

But about blushing.

The blush is often – but not always – a clue to guilt. When a small boy is guilty, he generally blushes. Not so his elders, who have acquired the antidote from habitual face-saving and profitable experience. Women are supposed to blush when praises are showered upon them. Some do, and some don't, while others are quite capable of acknowledging the compliment with a vicious lick of a handbag or an unexpected kick in the shin.

In many respects, a blush is a confession, although it is not acceptable evidence in a court of law. If we were to be convicted for our blushes, very few would emerge with a clean slate.

I may be totally wrong, but it seems to me that blushing is not as common as it used to be. Once upon a time if you told a girl of eighteen that a certain young gentleman was enamoured of her she would turn as red as a beetroot, but nowadays the news might be received with a smirk or the observation that he was a poor twister. Is it because youngsters aren't as shy as they used to be, and is it because teenage development is not as sheltered as it was? I am inclined to think so. There used to be great pleasure in telling a predictable chap of eighteen that a certain girl was enquiring about him. If he didn't blush, he was undoubtedly anaemic and when he did blush, it was interesting to speculate on the amount of time he devoted to dreaming of the particular girl. It was easy to guess from the extent of the facial area covered by the blush. Some blushes are like ripples. They spread downwards to the peak of the Adam's apple and sideways to the exposed patches behind the ears. I have no medical evidence at my disposal but I venture to state that the source of all blushes is the cheek. The blush is born here. The blush ends at the tip of the nose where it eventually expires.

I have seen men blushing when derogatory remarks were made about their forebears. This is the blush of indignation and should serve as a warning to those who provoke it. I was once witness to a rather peculiar phenomenon with regard to blushing. I saw a young bachelor of seventy blushing one spring morning years ago. When he thought nobody was watching he poured half a bottle of hair-oil over his sparsely-populated poll. When he saw that I was looking he blushed furiously like a schoolboy, recovered himself quickly, however, and winked at me mischievously out of the corner of his eye. The blush remained nonetheless and the hair-oil glistened on his head like dewdrops on a forsaken duck-egg.

While I do not condemn the artificial blush, its value is negligible because of its permanence. Make-up, particularly rouge, deceives nobody because a blush is an instant thing and dies almost at the moment of birth.

We often hear the expression: "Twould make a black man blush!' as if to intimate that the act which caused the blush was a very horrendous one indeed, but the truth is that black men blush as easily as white but only a black man knows when a black man is blushing.

A blush can be a very beautiful thing, and the true blush belongs on the face of innocence. It will be a sorry world when our young maidens no longer blush to remind us of our own young dreams and heartaches and to keep fresh the memory of innocent yesterdays.

I am wholeheartedly in favour of blushing. The man who has forgotten how to blush is a very hardened individual, a very wise fellow without doubt, but the man who blushes his way through life has a conscience and a soul and much of his youthful innocence has not yet deserted him.

Blushing brings to mind that beautiful song:

And soon my love will be my bride,
Sit blushing by my own fireside …

To all young brides, I wish a lifetime of blushing. That you might be blushing till the day you die, and that your sorrows and woes may be drowned in suffusion of your winsome blushes.

April 1963

Talkers

I once knew an actor who always included a few lines of his own whenever he got on the stage. He couldn't help it. He was a natural talker. It was always necessary to tie a piece of fishing-gut on to his trousers and to chuck it hard two or three times to remind him that it was time to give somebody else a chance.

Talking is a God-given gift and an incomparable means of communication. We often hear it said of a woman that she is a terrible talker. This does not mean that she is a nagger. Yapper would be a more descriptive word. This woman's husband generally has to wait a long time for his dinner. He doesn't complain, because he knows she really can't help it. He knows she is standing at some corner with her shopping bag in her hand bemoaning the state of the world with a colleague of the same bent. Her knew before he married her that she was an incurable talker, and this was one of the reasons why he pursued her. He liked to hear her chattering aimlessly about inconsequential things and her voice held a music for him that was to be found in no other. Her neighbours might say of her, 'God bless her, she'd talk the hind leg off a pot!' but for him the ceaseless murmur of her voice was a source of the greatest joy.

I have heard certain women referred to as talking machines. These can talk for any given length of time on any subject from any position you care to name. They can screw their heads around in buses and deliver marathon speeches to friends several seats away. They can lean out of upstairs windows at unbelievable angles and talk about astronauts or malt and cod liver oil. They can outline the progress of ecumenical councils and debate the outcome of unpredictable Munster finals. They live for talk and it is a strange fact that these women are married to men who prefer not to talk at all.

A truly talkative woman will talk under any circumstance. She will talk where it is forbidden to talk, but I believe that no woman should be restrained. I like talkative women. I like to listen to them and to savour the cadences and pitches of their women's voices. Often, in buses and trains, I have closed my eyes and listened while a woman's voice introduced me to unknown worlds of hats and blouses and shoes and I have convinced myself that there is a lot to be learned from listening regardless of the subject under discussion. I can close my eyes and hear of confirmation dresses and yellow party frocks and sometimes, if I'm lucky, I hear incredible descriptions of model husbands and even though I know there isn't an ounce of truth in them, my heart is on the side of the woman who paints a rosy picture of her own dear partner.

Sometimes we are not disposed to listen to talk and there is an infuriating type who has no regard for the privacy of others. He butts into conversations and contributes opinions where none are wanted. He proceeds, after getting a leg in, to monopolise the conversation.

There are others, peculiar to trains and buses, who introduce themselves to total strangers and keep up an irritating flow until the victim is obliged to depart his seat or compelled to tell the intruder to shut up and go away. It is no use pretending to be asleep because the sworn talker is generally contaminated with a voice like a rasp.

I cannot stand loud and obstreperous talkers or, if you like aggressive talkers. These are usually to be found in public houses and they generally manage to unsettle the composure of peaceable drinkers so that the pub is no longer a place of retreat. But an old gentleman who owned a county pub was master of occasions like these. He was the possessor of an old gramophone which he turned on whenever a vainglorious and fight-seeking shouter got out of hand.

There are other quieter types of men who like to talk to themselves. I don't know why some people think it peculiar that other people should talk to themselves. I often talk to myself, sometimes contentedly and other times contentiously. There's many a man who likes to praise himself and on the other hand to deride himself because there is nobody sufficiently interested in him to care whether he deserves praise or blame for his way of living. Some less endearing types talk to themselves all the time even when they are being addressed by others. There was an old man I knew who talked to himself all the time. He was asked one day by a curious young fellow why he persisted in talking to himself all the while. 'Because I never met a nicer fellow than myself,' the old man replied, 'and I'm also the best listener I know.'

Sometimes, after rows in the home, and outside it, the protagonists do not talk to each other at all for long periods. In the home, this is a good thing because it frequently provides a breathing space or lull which is very necessary where people are eternally conscious of each other. Outside the home it is foolish and cruel and it is always painful to hear of people who don't talk to each other. It is misusing the power of speech and it is a root cause of indigestion and neuralgia. It passes from one generation to another and, in time, although the breach is not healed, a man forgets his reasons for not talking to another man, so if there's someone to whom you're not talking, put it off no longer. Bid him the time o' day the next time you meet and as sure as there's meat on the shin of a wren, it won't be long before you'll be talking.

June 1963

The Lipstick on our Glasses

Two lips, whose beauty in my heart
I feel when we are far apart;
Two lips, where I shall find always
Repose from weary nights and days.

There are more foreign bodies to be found in public house glasses than you'd find in a battlefield of the first crusade.

They are a source of constant concern to the conscientious barman and reputations were often lost on the strength of unexpected impurities.

An acquaintance of mine once called for a pint of stout in a country pub where the proprietor was easy-going and difficult to impress. The pint was duly filled and placed on the counter. My acquaintance noticed that a dead wasp lay on the surface of the pint. He called the proprietor and pointed at the corpse. The proprietor dipped his finger into the glass and withdrew the wasp. My acquaintance grinned his disapproval.

'I don't know what's the matter with you,' the proprietor said. 'First you wouldn't drink it with the wasp in it, and now you won't drink it with the wasp out!'

The wasp, if he had shown any consideration for my friend, might have chosen a less public place for his lying-in-state, but the question I am forced to ask is: 'Have we grown too particular about the manner in which our drinks are served?'

It is my contention that we have. I am all for hygiene but

too much of it induces mental sterility and soon a man will be forced to wash his hands before he swallows his porter.

I have seen men on the verge of hysteria because they discovered lipstick stains on the rims of their glasses. Others have crowed with delight and said nothing whatsoever. When barmen and barmaids are busy, it is not always easy to spot lipstick stains, especially if the shades are light and airy like tee-pink, rose pink and pale pink.

When I come across a smear of lipstick on my glass I drink from the other side if the people back of the counter are run off their feet and I try to conjure up the style of woman who drank out of the glass before me.

Ice-pink generally means a bottle of orange crush for a teenager. Rose pink is inevitably a sherry for a maid in her early twenties, but tangerine and pink-with-a-wink are probably gins and bitter lemons. These latter, too, are laden with intrigue and it is hard to assess the characters of the damsels who down them.

I have little interest in natural pink, but I am open to correction. However, it appears to me that natural pinks lack dash and colour and are possible drinkers of bottled stout for imaginary anaemia or high-fangled nervous disorders.

The shade that has me fooled is orange floss. It brings to mind a charming miller's daughter with ringlets and blushing cheeks, but I was fooled lately because I came across an orange floss who was a rum and coke and not the peppermint that I expected.

Orange floss could be anything from soda water to advocaat and ginger ale, and some years ago in Ballybunion during my bachelor days I got the land of my life when, after the third dance, two lips well-primed with orange floss announced that they would, indeed, accept my invitation for a drink. At the time I had 4/6 in my pocket, and to increase my misfortunes, my lovely partner had that most disarming of charms, a back-from-England accent.

We went out in the cool night air and entered a nice little bar where a rousing sing-song was in progress. I asked her what she fancied, and without as much as a blush, she calmly demanded a snipe of champagne. Luckily, I got in touch with the barman while she went to powder her nose, and he convinced her upon her return, that there were no such things as snipes of champagne to be had in such an unpretentious place as Ballybunion.

I kept away from orange flosses after that, or at least from orange flosses with contrary thirsts. On the other hand, you could meet with an orange floss who drinks nothing but milk, but my advice to bachelors with limited means is – don't chance it. You're better off with an orange-loving ice-pink, although to the tell the truth, there is only the same certainty about a shade of lipstick as there is about a shade of woman.

Once upon a time, you would travel a hundred pubs and you would be hard put to find a glass with lipstick on it. Today no pub is free from lipstick. I am not condemning lipstick or the delightful creatures who sport it. I am all for women who do all in their power to beautify themselves, but it can be embarrassing when a pernickety customer demands his money back because he is allergic to lipstick.

Bikini pink is impossible to discover on long ornate lager glasses, where racing red is sticking out a mile on all kinds of glasses. Cool mango I don't trust an inch, but don't ask me why. In the days of sowing the oats, I never came across a cool mango, whereas I have blissful memories of Bermuda coral.

Whenever I see vivid red on the rim of an unwashed glass, I am reminded of deliriously happy times and climes. This shade is not so familiar any more, but I remember how my bride bought a tube of it on the afternoon of our wedding day.

Truthfully, of course, it is not lipstick that matters but the lips underneath it, and I daresay that lipstick enhances rather than classifies. A glass with no trace of lipstick on it at all may be more unhygienic than a host of stained glasses, so the next time you find lipstick on your glass, pause for a moment and try to picture the creature who put it there. Studies of this kind can be rewarding and if, sadly enough, you happen to be one of those who cannot stand the sight of lipstick on your glass, don't complain too loudly because, who knows, it may be somebody you know quite well – your neighbour, your sister or even your mother.

Aug 1963

On Going Grey

Over the past few months, a large number of grey hairs have come to pay their respects on my thatch.

Obviously, they were impressed by their surroundings, for word has gone out to friends and relatives and now they are making their first bid to wrest the original colour from my cranium.

I discovered my first grey hair several years ago, but he was before his time and he did not stay long. Others came after him, in ones and twos, but they, too, declined to stay. They were totally outnumbered, for one thing, and they lacked the pioneering spirit of true colonists, for another.

Most ambitious young men have nothing against a touch of grey, as long as it stops at a touch. It implies maturity and many youthful professional men pray for the arrival of grey hairs in the hope that they will bring standing and seniority.

I am not in the least worried about growing grey, that is, totally grey. If you can't lick 'em, join 'em, is my motto in this respect and, anyhow, we are told that grey is a colour which goes with everything. It is a natural shade.

The first grey hair should not be regarded as an insidious ambassador on the make. He should be welcomed and made much of, for his bridgeheads are made without pain or bloodshed and his final victory accomplished without the humility of unconditional surrender.

Some men – and some women, too – grow grey before their time because of hereditary or other natural phenomena.

Still, I have often heard of a child being born with a silver spoon in his mouth, but I have never heard of one with grey hair on his head. The advice I offer to the prematurely grey is this: Be glad, because you could be prematurely bald.

Man thinks it imperative that his women be wooed and wed before grey hairs usurp the glistening bristles of his thatch. Alas, this is not so wise because most women like a man with a touch of grey over his ears. Greyness is relative any way you look at it and so long as the greyness doesn't eat its way into the heart, it is acceptable.

But how shall I come to the female side of it? This is a touchy subject because women like to keep grey hairs at bay indefinitely. They tend to pluck grey hairs, in defiance of the legend which says that for every grey hair plucked eight more will grow in its stead. I do not credit this, but I do not dismiss it either because anxiety about approaching greyness is a sure way of hastening grey hairs.

Many women do not wait for nature to do its work: they take the bull by the horns and choose their own shades of grey at 3/6d. a bottle. Blue grey, charcoal grey and steel grey are the popular shades, but far-seeing women take their chances with home-mixed tints, even if the end result is off-white.

Others who refuse to admit to natural changes manage to present an outstanding range of changing colours to a world which refuses to be astonished by anything any more. Greens, blues and yellows have illuminated the hatless heads of females who have a flair for living, a desire to be different and who conduct crusades for personal recognition.

Let us have more of these women and more of these colours. Let those who carp and criticise look to their own heads, for

Throwing One's Weight About

Throwing one's weight around is invariably successful and a thick neck is worth a ton of talent.

The world acknowledges the man who pushes himself. People get out of his way not because they are intimidated but because they wish to avoid embarrassment. There is a weight-thrower in every queue and it's odds on that he'll jump it at the expense of others. It is all a matter of making one's presence felt so as to secure an audience or to gain an advantage.

A retired sprint jockey entered a public house and loudly banged on the counter.

'Two glasses of whiskey,' he shouted at the barman, 'and see that it is whiskey, pie-face.'

'My name isn't pie-face,' the barman, who was a man of sixteen stone, said.

'Don't rile me,' the sprint jockey, who was four feet seven, said, 'or I'm liable to cut loose.'

Indulgently, the barman filled the two glasses of whiskey, and sat on his stool, perplexed. After a while, the jockey took a mouse from his pocket. He handed the mouse a glass of whiskey and together they drained the contents of both glasses. The mouse, who had an irritating voice, began to sing and customers began to leave the bar.

'Can't you do anything with that mouse?' the barman pleaded.

'Go to hell!' said the jockey.

'That's right,' said the mouse, 'and if there's a cat in the house he can go to hell too!'

The moral of the story is that a mouse with a bit of neck can get away with murder.

Each of us has experienced an incidence of weight-throwing and each of us has lost face because we were too afraid of attracting notice and more afraid of improbable consequences. I have seen it myself in shops and dining-rooms. A man of consequence enters and assistants fall over each other to dance attendance upon him. Regular customers are suddenly forgotten and regular customers, to their everlasting shame, accept the situation.

I remember, only last year, a friend and I returned to our hotel having visited a few taverns in the city. The receptionist told my friend that she had removed his bags and put them in another room.

'But I can't sleep in that room,' he protested, 'the morning traffic wakes me too early.'

'I'm sorry,' she said, 'but it's Mr So-and-So' (mentioning a well-known figure).

'And do you know who I am?' my friend countered.

The receptionist shook her head.

'I am a direct descendent of Adam and Eve, as Mr Keane here will testify, so kindly put my bags back in my room or I shall do so myself.'

Ever since that time I have always seen to it that I, myself, have got a fair crack of the whip. There are far too many people who throw their weight about. I know that, in the beginning, any time I protested about preferential treatment the result was acute embarrassment, and the only person upset by the situation was myself, but nowadays I get a great personal satisfaction from demanding my rights. I feel that I am doing a favour to myself and others but particularly to people who are always kept waiting because they haven't the neck to speak up.

Unusually dressed people or people with affected accents generally manage to command attention, and this is perhaps the most subtle of all the forms of throwing one's weight about. Their appearances do the pushing for them and they are well aware of the effect they create. That is why they adopt out-landish modes of dress and unusual attitudes of behaviour.

At the entrance to a football field a long queue stood waiting for the gates to open. Many had been there since morn-ing to assure themselves of a good view. A slightly-built, be-spectacled man was at the head of the queue, but when the gates opened, an aggressive man with a red face pushed him out of the way and took his place.

'I beg your pardon –' the bespectacled man said with justifiable outrage.

'Small states shouldn't threaten Russia,' the queue-jum-per shouted, and with that he disappeared into the grounds.

There is another moral here. If you must stand at the head of a queue, you must also carry a darning needle in your lapel. Another question arises, however. Is there a psycho-logical defence against queue-jumpers? The answer is in the negative, since one can expect no assistance from other queue members, who are, naturally, worried about their own places. A good idea is to choose the largest man in the crowd and to point him out to offenders as your brother. Failing that, a good kick in the shin can be effective.

If anything, women are worse for throwing their weight about than men. Some women want to be wherever there is excitement, and will stop at nothing to achieve their ends. They begin by pushing their husbands about and end up by thinking they can push everybody else. They start off by imposing themselves on societies and social groups, but that isn't enough because they need special prestige as well. They like to be seen with famous people, and display unbelievable ignorance in their approach. They tell people how to hold parties and stick their noses in where they are not wanted. Their voices are loud and their manners abominable. They snub people and hurt people, but let us all be consoled because they are never happy since there is no end to their ambitions.

So long as people continue to be courteous and kind there will be weight-throwers to take advantage of them, but it is wise to remember that there is a not too distant place where the slightest sign of throwing one's weight about would result in a permanent stand at the end of the line.

Oct 1963

Making Faces

Did you ever make a face at a person, only to have that person turn suddenly around and catch you fair and square in the act?

An awkward situation, and one in which most of us have been uncompromisingly placed at one time or another.

The best instance of caught-in-the-act face-making I remember happened some years ago while a party of us were journeying in a bus to a certain village. Before we had a chance to alight, a burly barger of a woman forced herself on to the bus and caused no little commotion. When the conductor tried to forestall her, she stuck out her tongue at him and she wasn't in the least embarrassed when he caught her in the act.

'Are you from this village, ma'am?' the conductor asked.

'I am!' she said. 'What about it?'

'Well,' said the conductor, 'the last woman that stuck out her tongue in these parts had it stolen out of her gob by her neighbours.'

Making faces at people when their backs are turned is not a commendable practice, even if it is sometimes necessary. When a big man berates a small man, the small man may grin and glare with impunity when his tormentor's back is turned, but he must be quick about it and be ready with a look of angelic innocence should the big man turn in a hurry. It is justifiable because it is the only means of redress at the little man's disposal.

Making faces at good-looking girls is face-making of another sort altogether and a pastime which I heartily endorse. I might ask what exactly is a face for, apart from its being admired by its owner. The eyes are for looking, the ears are for hearing, the nose for smelling and the mouth for eating, but what about the rest of it – the cheeks, the beauty spots, the dimples and so on. The rest, of course, is for making faces – not unpleasant faces but faces which excite pity or admiration, concern or love.

The best people for making these types of faces are young ladies of marriageable age. The faces they make are part of their natural assets and many a young man was driven to distraction at the sight of the barest frown on a certain incomparable face.

The lips – which I almost overlooked – are for kissing – although I have read in romantic novels of young chaps who kiss girls on the nose and chin. Certain authorities hold that these Romeos should have their noggins examined for who is going to bother with a nose or a chin when he has a pair of willing lips at his disposal.

An elderly man (he was a bachelor) once told me that matrimonially-inclined young ladies spend hours practising faces in front of mirrors. I cannot vouch for this but there may be something in it, particularly when one hears of girls with such quaint and wistful looks of startled innocence that impressionable young men were tempted on the spur of the moment to offer permanent protection in the form of unpremeditated proposals.

I know for a fact that girls practice smiling in an effort to determine the type best suited to their faces. In many respects, it's like choosing a hat to go with a new outfit because smile styles must change with hairstyles and no woman is satisfied with a permanent smile. Be that as it may, but don't forget that smiles are of permanent importance, for when a dour spouse after a rift with his helpmate remembers a particular smile she bestowed upon him in their days of courtship, his heart melts with tenderness and remorse when he recalls a slim and trusting girl of yesterday.

Young men who have been spurned often resort to face-making as a means of cajoling the desired one into changing her mind. This practice has been known to produce the required result when properly executed but let me stress the danger of over-playing the part. A pale face and red-rimmed eyes is a combination which has been known to work but pulling one's hair over one's eyes and frothing at the mouth is a trifle too exaggerated and can only result in total rejection. I heard of a young man who puffed out his cheeks and extended his lower dentures over his lower lip with the result that the poor girl fainted. He was later prosecuted by the father and sentenced to fourteen days without option.

Making faces during courtroom trials is an art without parallel. The most astute of judges have time and again been taken in by the truly accomplished rogue. One of the greatest impostors I ever knew went into the box with his rosary beads draped over his fingers and the look of a martyred saint on his face. When the prosecution went into the attack with the final unanswerable accusation the defendant burst out crying, so much so that the kindly justice reprimanded the unfortunate prosecutor and dismissed the case on the merits.

The face I enjoy most of all is that put on by the timid

man when danger threatens. If he is a good actor, he can frighten the wits out of his adversaries. If, in addition, he can growl or grind his teeth the entire presentation can be most intimidating, but the danger here is that if he sees his own face without warning in the mirror he might easily frighten the life out of himself.

Nov 1963

Hot-tempered Women

Are red-haired women hot-tempered?

I ask the question although I know the answer is that red-haired women are no more hot-tempered than black-haired, brown-haired or blonde-haired women.

I don't know a great deal about red-haired women. I am married to a woman with dark brown hair. In 1948, I took a red-haired woman to a dance in Newcastle West. Strictly speaking, I did not take her to the dance. Five of us, of the same age group, hired a car between us and it was more or less taken for granted that this red-haired girl and myself were to be partners for the night.

As things turned out it so happened that we were. She was a useful waltzer which means that she was far better than I. All in all, I found her of the same disposition and temperament as black-haired and blonde-haired women. In all fairness, I must say that she was an admirable companion. I am told that she is now happily married in New Jersey, the mother of three children and an asset to her husband who began life as a bellboy and is now a sub-contractor of standing in foundations.

I have questioned a number of men who have taken red-haired women for wives and I have found them strangely reluctant in admitting temperament or idiosyncrasies in their partners.

Personally speaking, I have no time at all for women without tempers. This statement may make me enemies but then a woman without a temper is not much of an enemy. I believe a woman who has never smashed a cup or flung a wet towel at her mate is biologically deficient and emotionally indifferent.

She who has not once in her lifetime thrown caution together with stew to the winds is lacking in abandon and is totally subject to the increasing demands of an overconfident husband.

She is without regard for the natural and legal rights of womanhood and if there is a return to the awful state of anti-suffragette, women without tempers will shoulder the major share of the responsibility.

Hot-tempered women are not on the way out, thank God, at least not to my knowledge, for there are daily reports of breakages and minor assaults.

Some time ago, a friend of mine told me that a quiet woman is worse than a nagging woman. When I asked him for a little clarification, he told me that quiet women get under a man's skin and demoralise him with silence. I do not subscribe to his view because all women, quiet or noisy, given enough time will talk.

When I speak about hot-tempered women, I do not mean women who threaten to leave their home, or to call in the brother-in-law, nor do I refer to women who bang doors noisily. Banging doors is not enough.

While discussing this same subject only last night, a husband of twenty years standing told me that in his second year of marriage his wife threw the following articles at him when he came home drunk on two successive nights:

One alarm clock;
One pint bottle of liquid paraffin;
One jar of zinc and castor-oil cream;
Two pairs of size four shoes;
One hot water bottle;
One full baby's bottle;
One framed picture of the wedding group;
Two vases (presents from his mother) and finally;
One electric heater.

Now there's my idea of a hot-tempered woman, a bit too hot-tempered maybe, but our friend never came home drunk on two successive nights again. None of the articles struck him because she did not shoot to kill. She managed to make her position clear, however, in no uncertain fashion. Most husbands have experienced isolated incidents of cup-throwing and jug-throwing. Many have had basins and dishcloths flung at them but these little incidents serve only to remind us that while our partners may look submissive and docile on the outside, underneath they are never really tamed. This is a good thing for what good is a tamed woman around a house?

There are some who will insist that their wives do not throw things. Old wives rarely throw things but young wives worth their salt do. To those of you who believe that your little darlings are meek and submissive, I offer the following gale-warning. Do not invite home drunken companions after closing time or you will get a suck-in. No matter how quiet a woman is, if she is made of the right stuff she will always rise to the occasion. I know a timid woman who flung an electric iron out of the front window at one o'clock in the morning, and another quiet soul who, after several submissive years, let her husband have it on the back of the head with her electric hair-dryer. I do not condone perpetual barrages but every marriage needs at least one onslaught with heavy artillery. To those who disagree with me, I say – wake up and live! When you're old and grey, there will be great sport in reminiscing about the sometime frenzy of a hot-tempered but delightful young woman.

Nov 1963